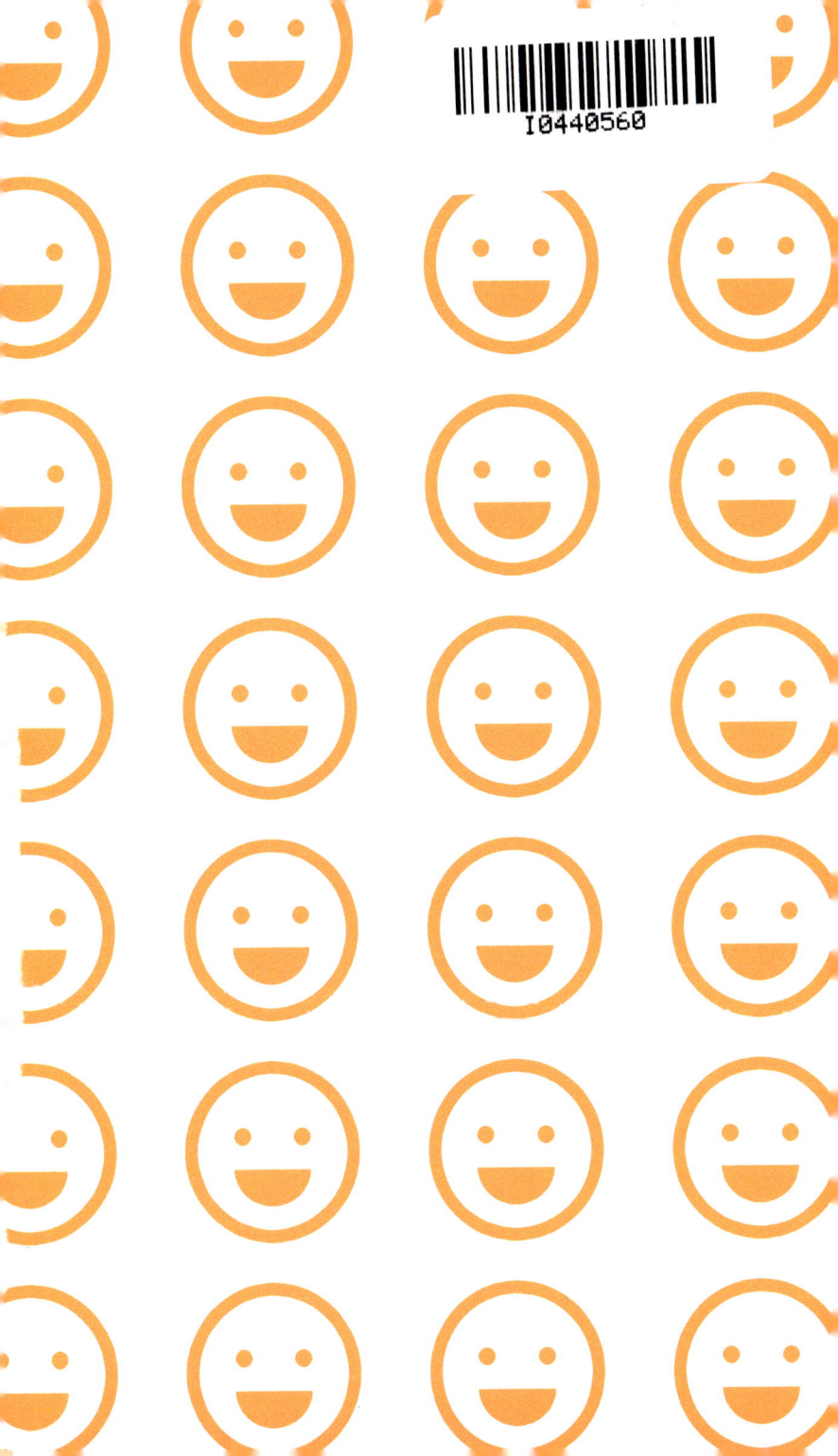

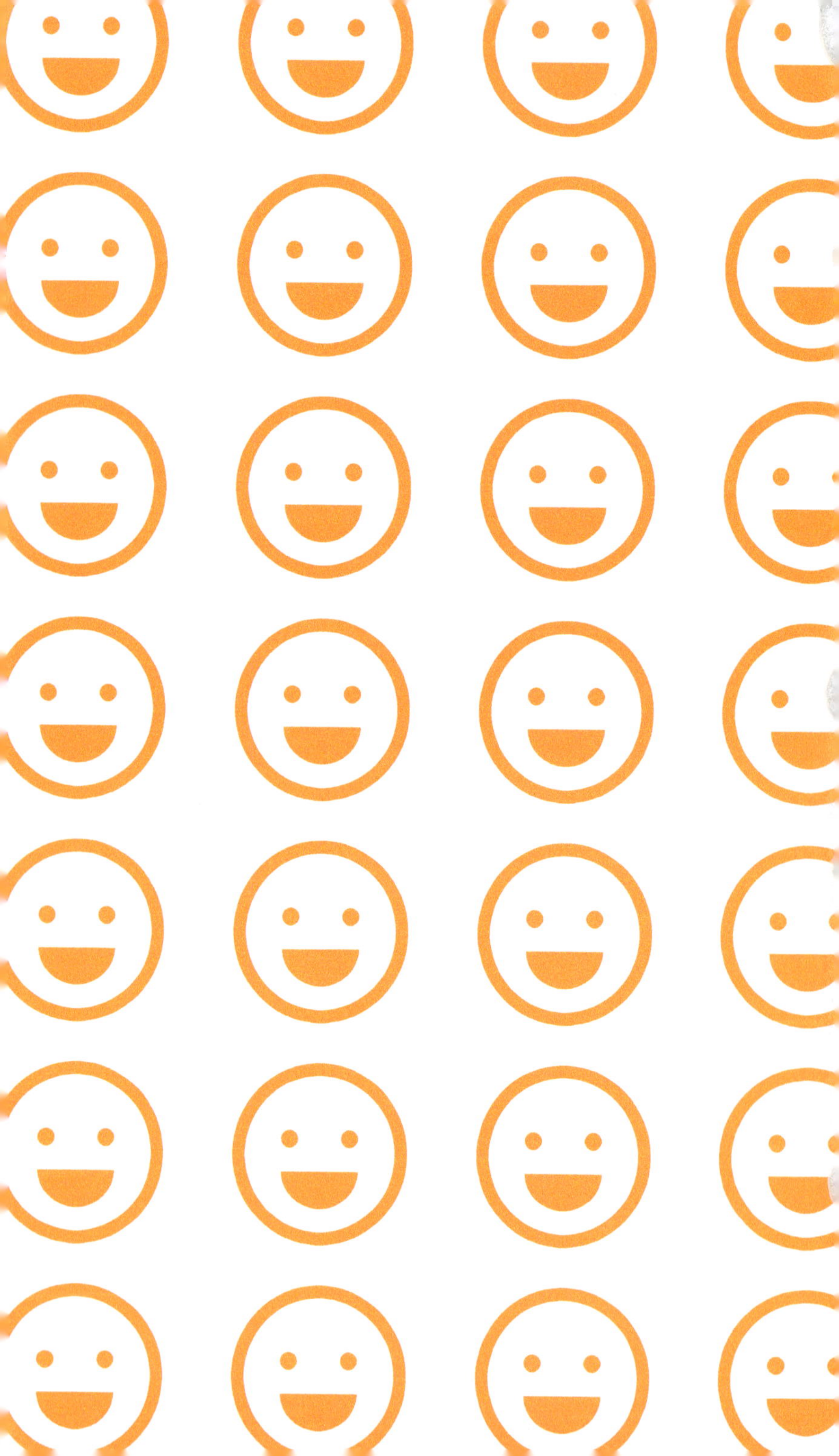

DRIVE FAST DON'T STOP

BOOK SEVEN

NEW YORK AUTO SHOW
2011-2019

FAST DON

FAST DON'

E FAST DON'T

VE FAST DON'T S

RIVE FAST DON'T STO

DRIVE FAST DON'T STOP

DRIVE FAST DON'T STOP

FAST DON'

FAST DON'T

E FAST DON'T

VE FAST DON'T ST

RIVE FAST DON'T STO

DRIVE FAST DON'T STOP

DRIVE FAST DON'T STOP

NEW YORK
NEW YORK
NEW YORK
NEW YORK
NEW YORK
NEW YORK
NEW YORK

AUTO SHOW
AUTO SHOW
AUTO SHOW
AUTO SHOW
AUTO SHOW
AUTO SHOW
AUTO SHOW

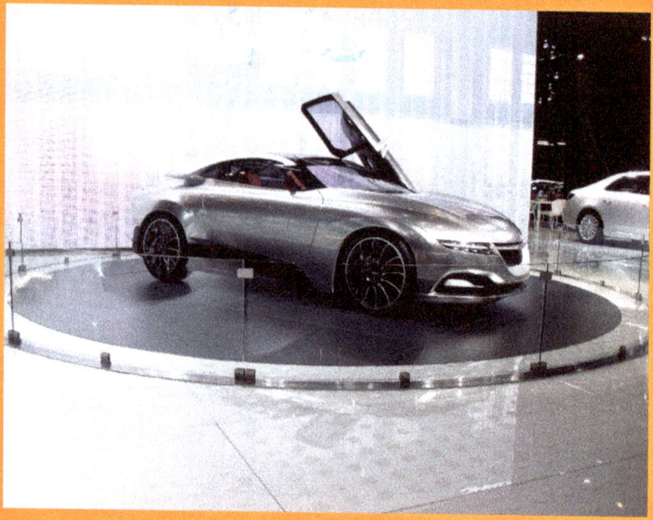

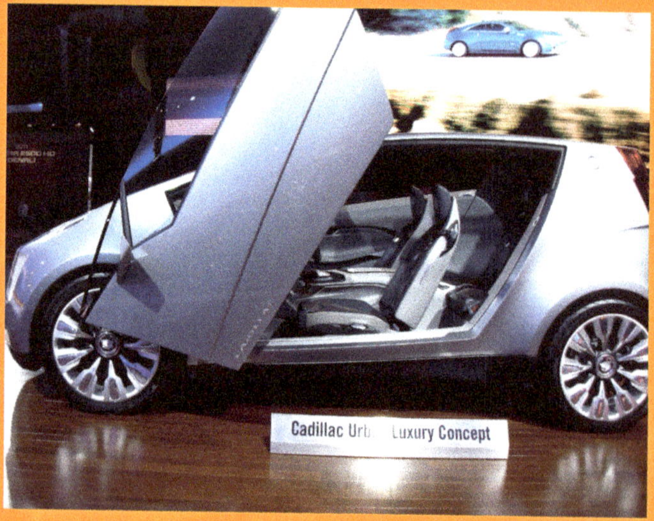
Cadillac
Luxury Concept

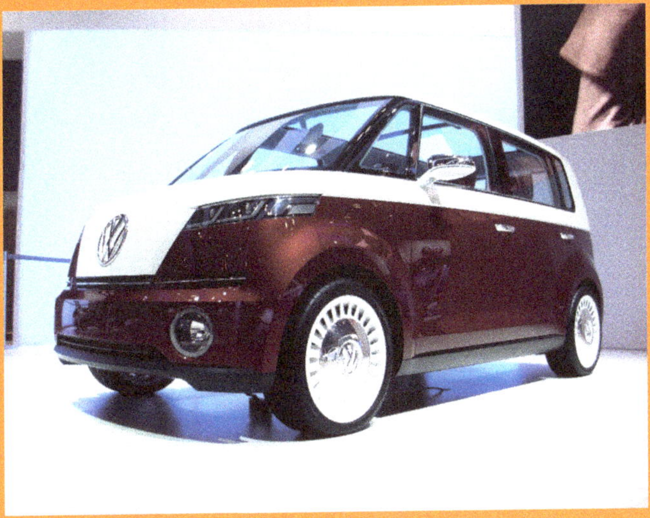

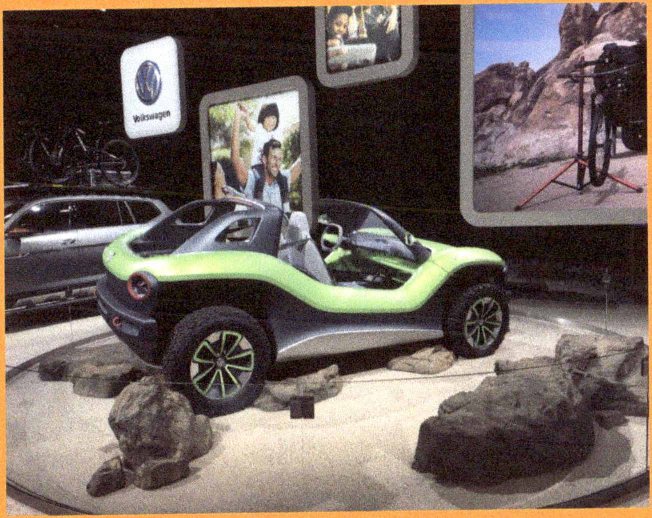
Volkswagen

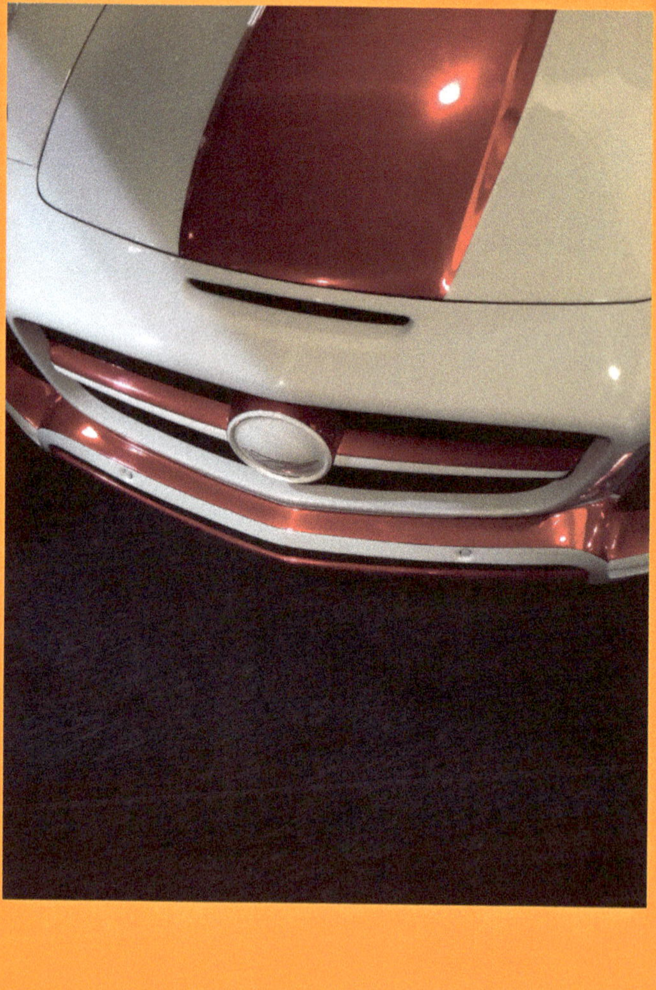

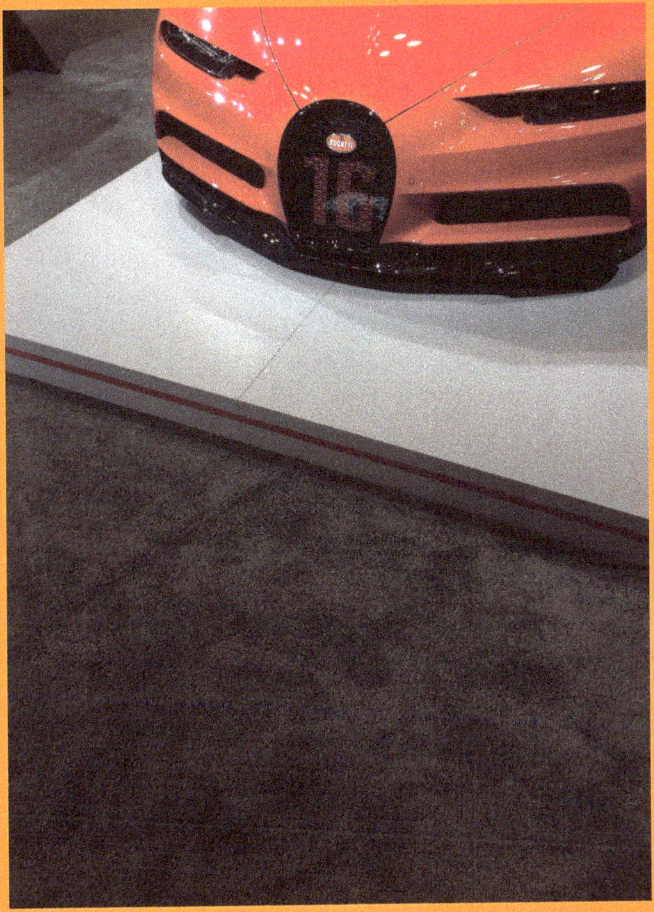
16

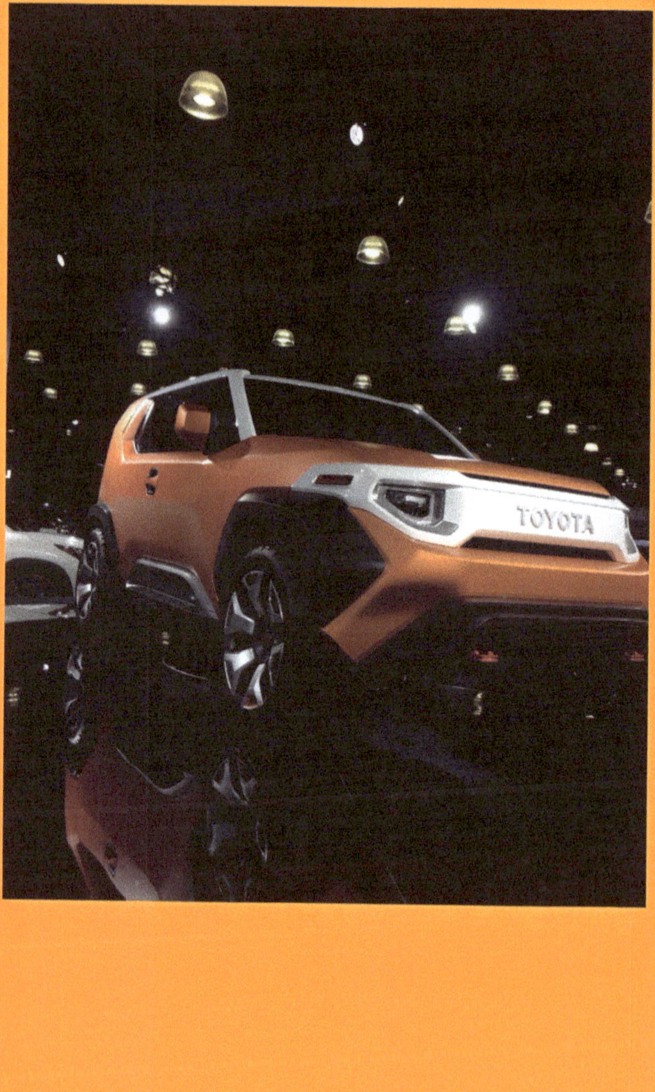
TOYOTA

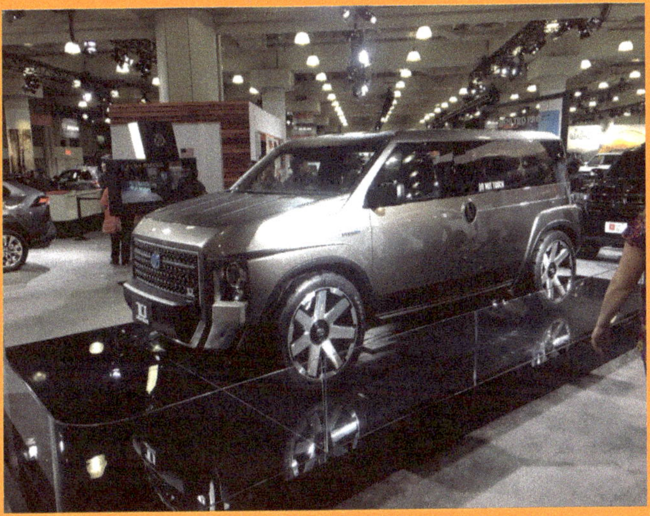

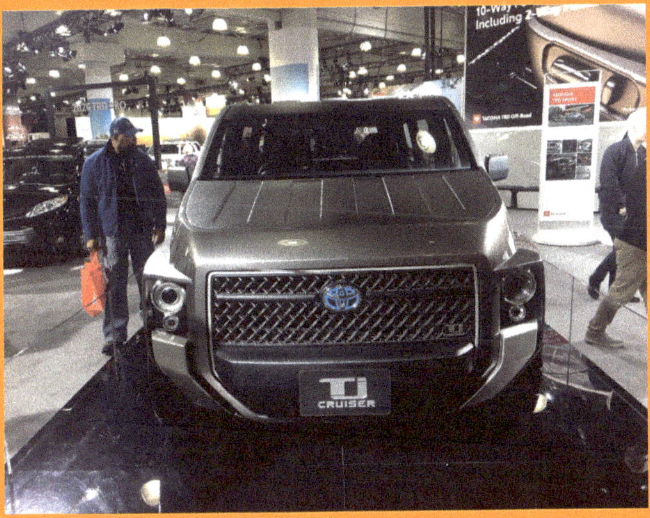
TJ
CRUISER

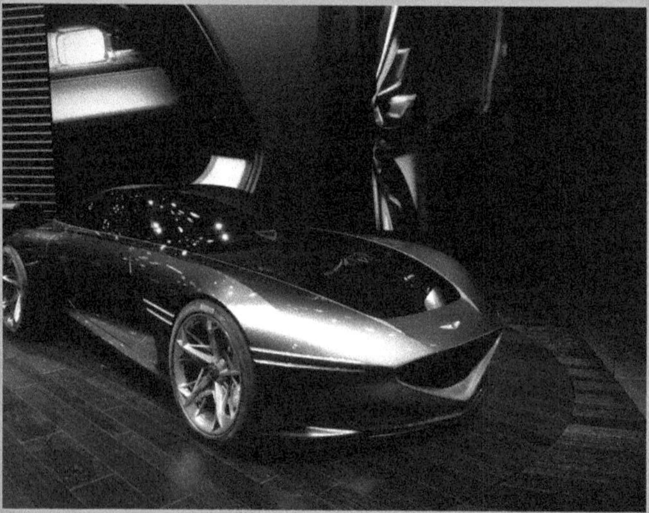

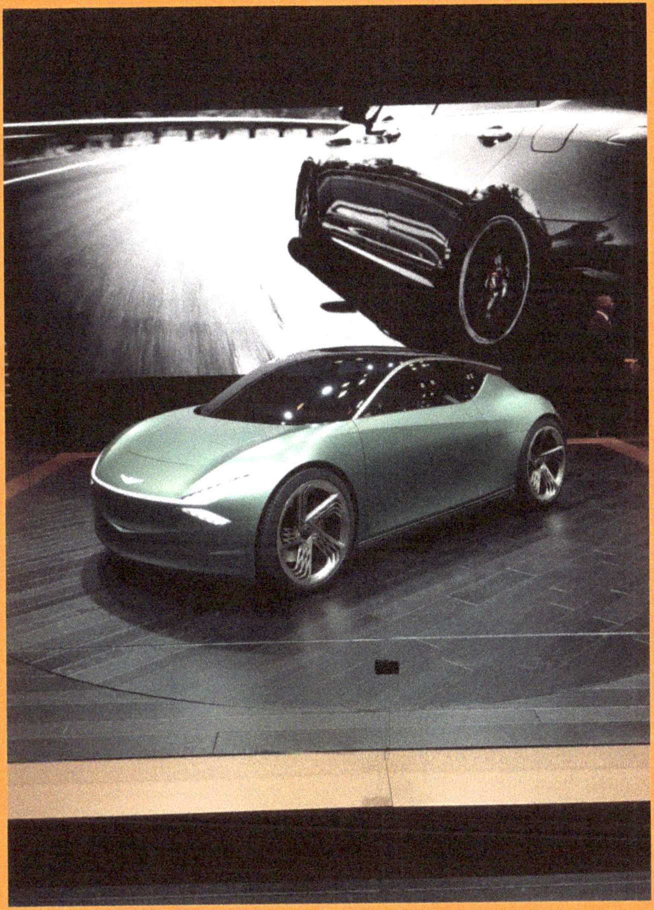

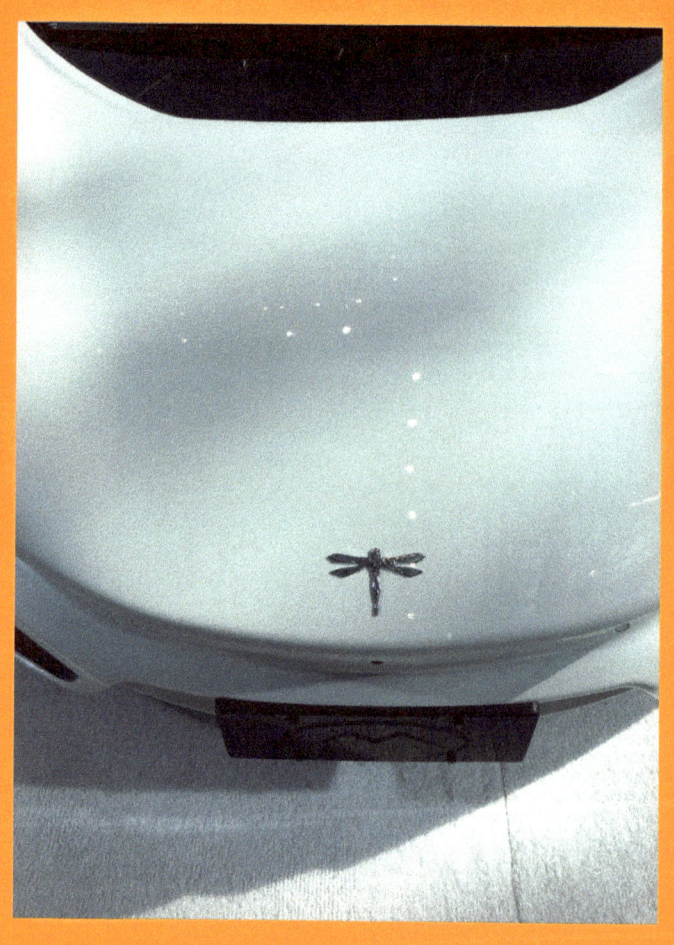

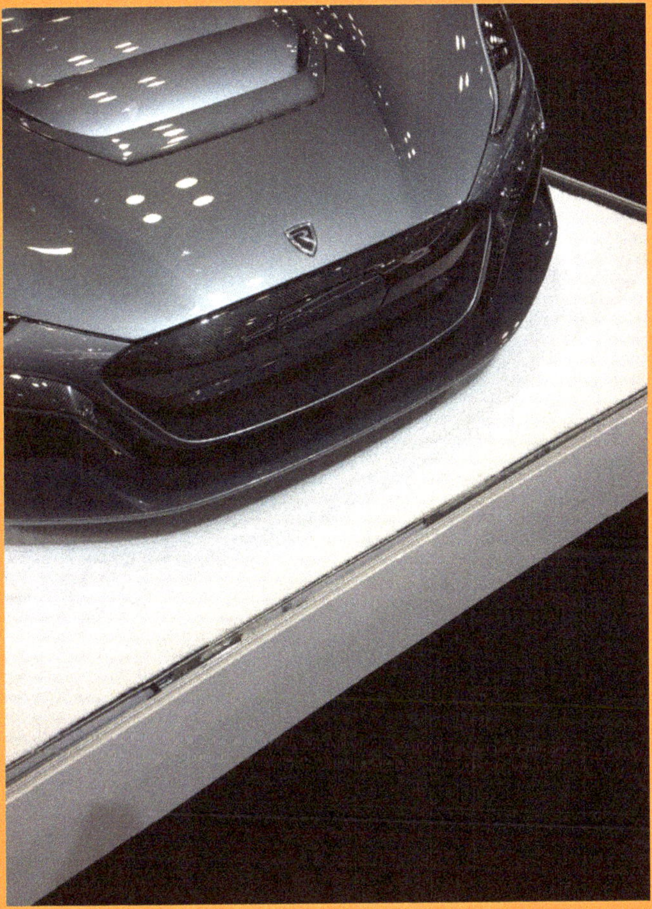

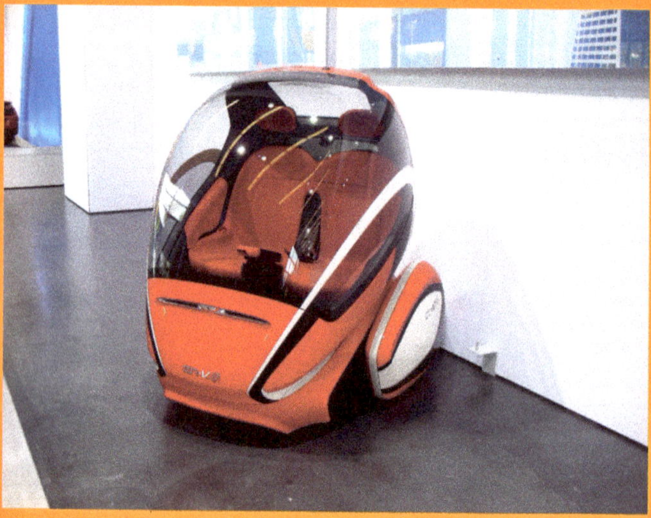

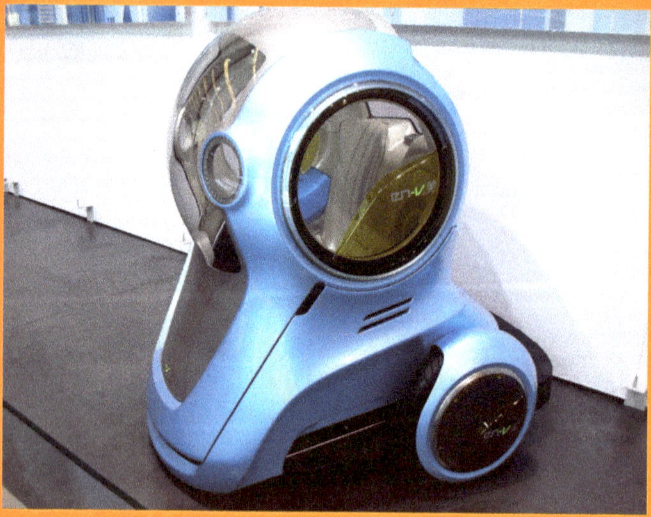

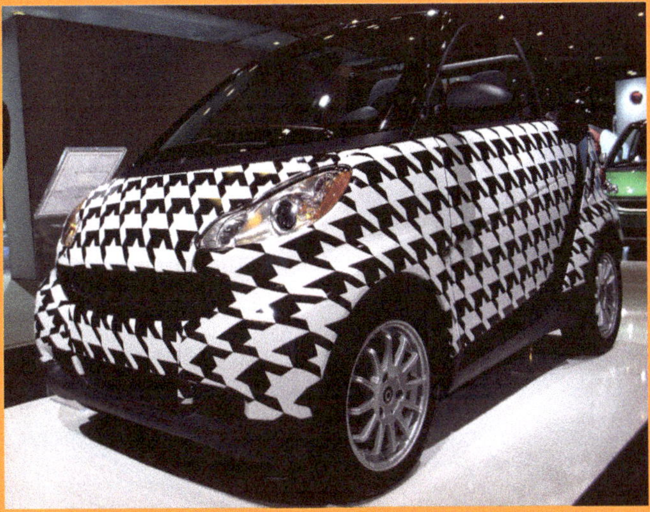

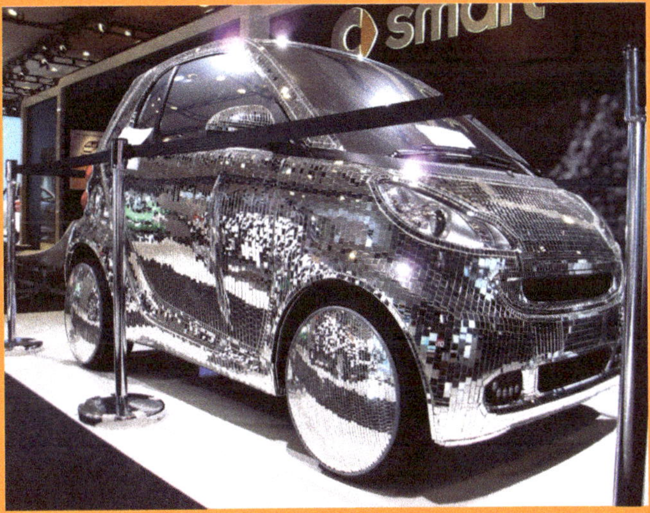

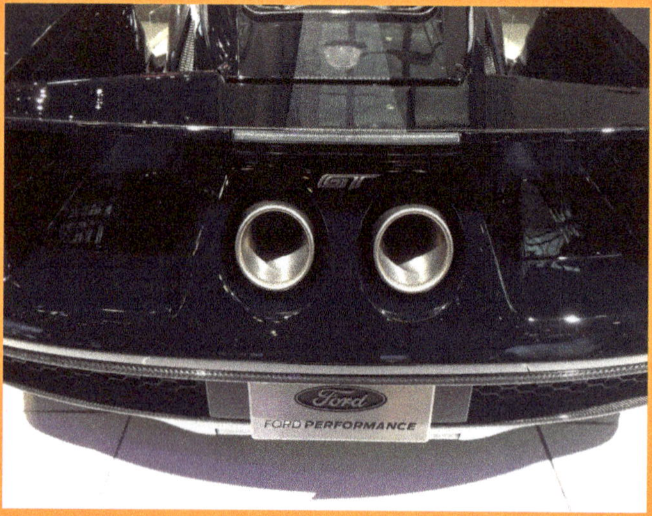
GT
Ford
FORD PERFORMANCE

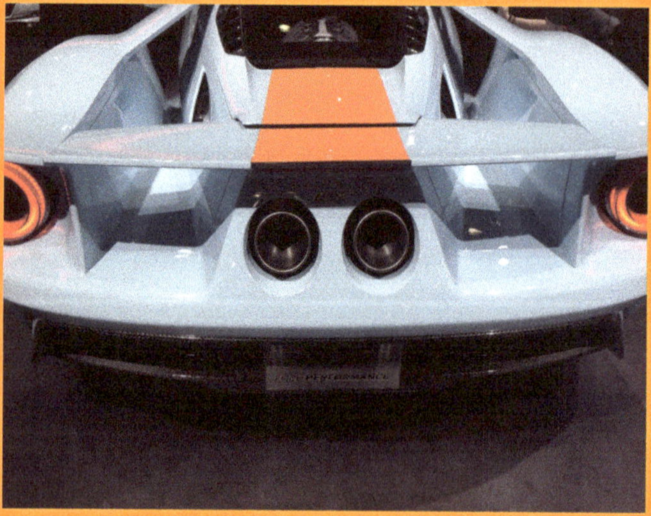

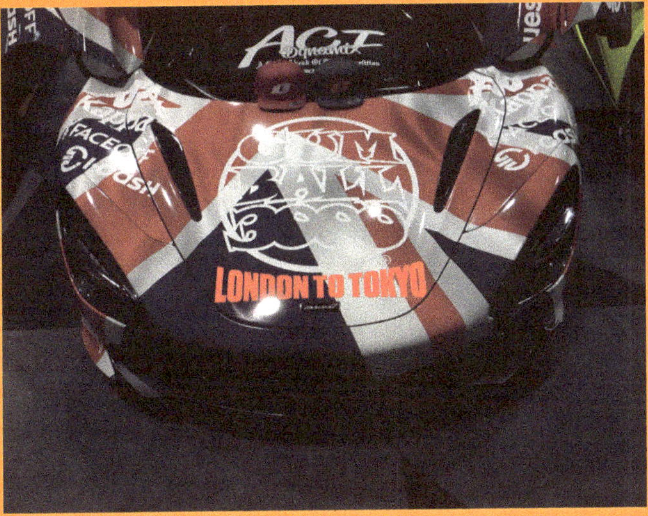
LONDON TO TOKYO

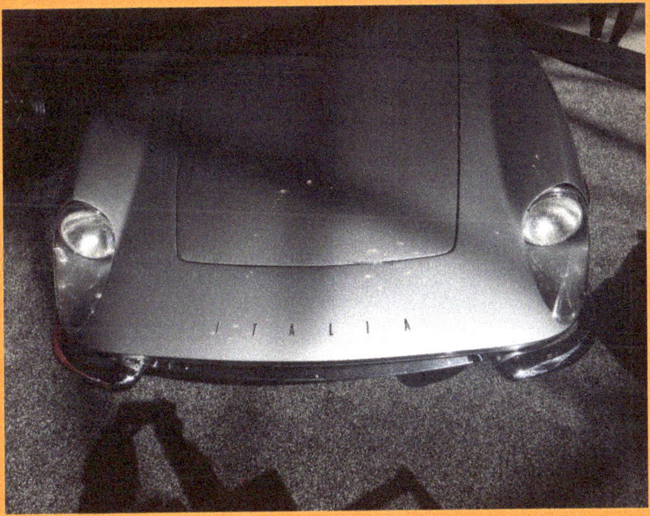
I T A L I A

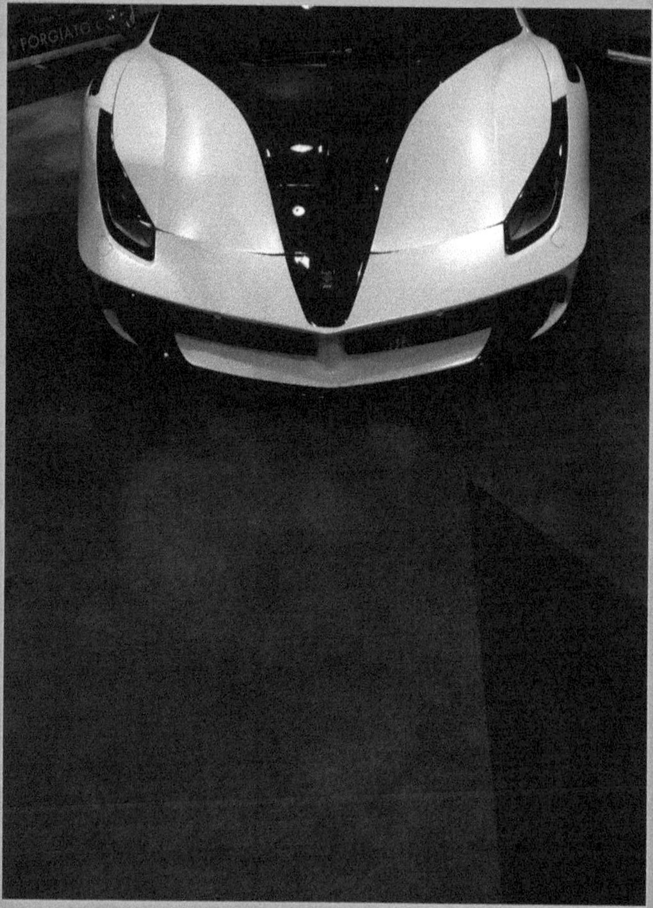
FORGIATO

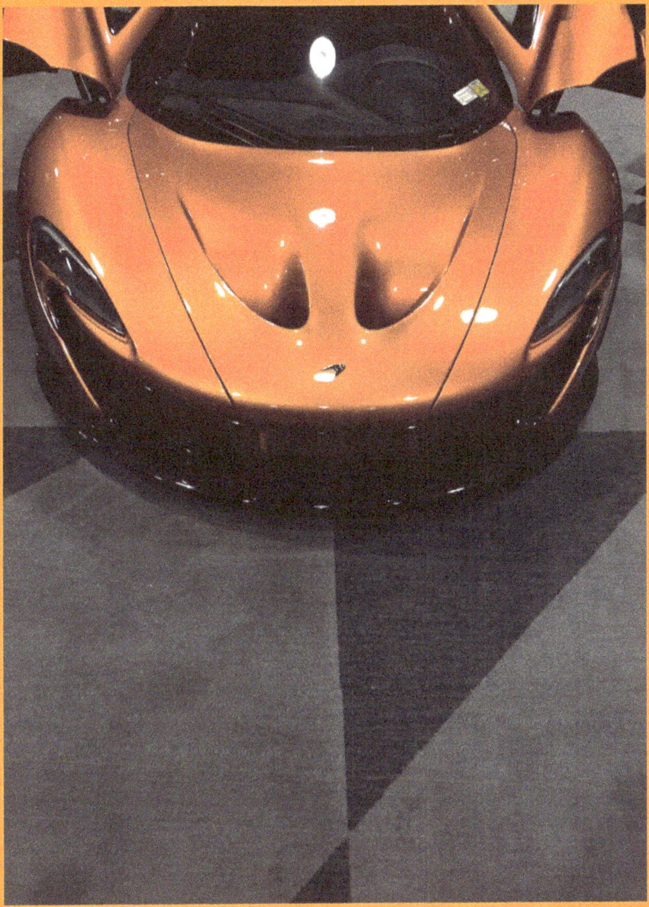

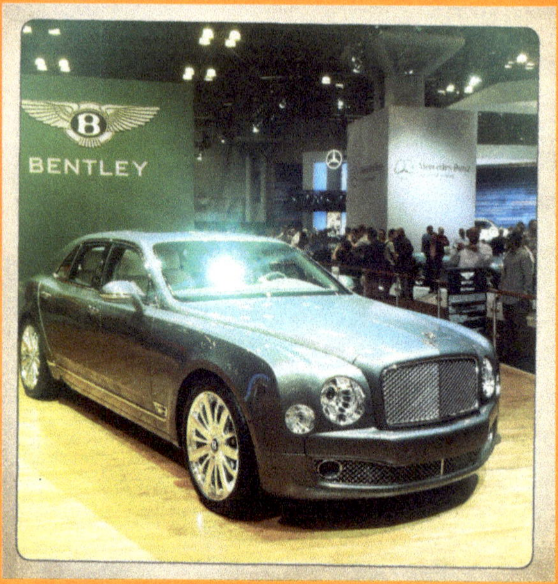
BENTLEY

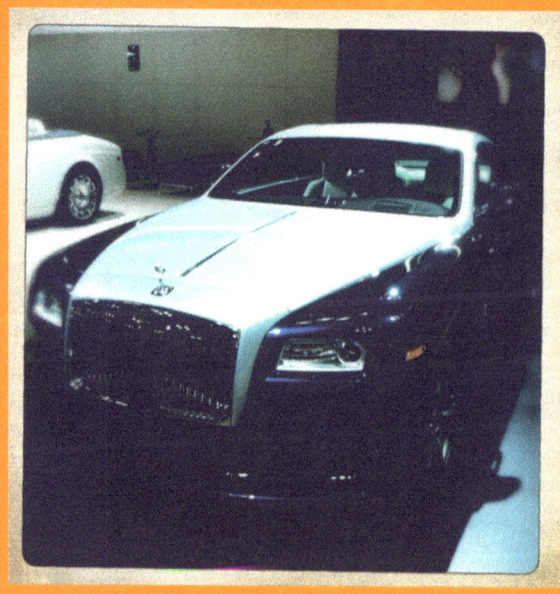

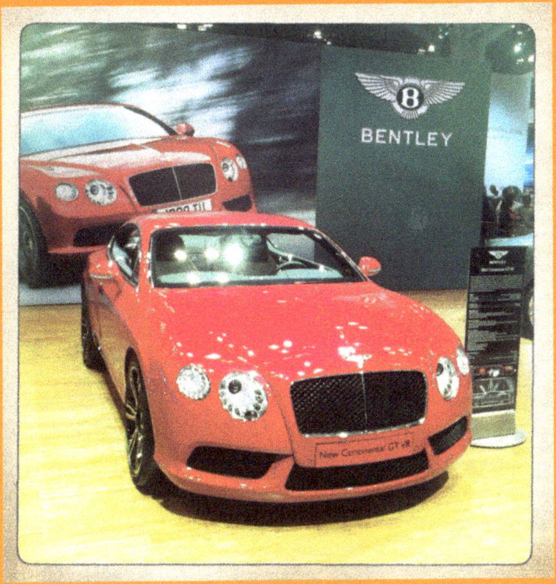
BENTLEY
New Continental GT V8

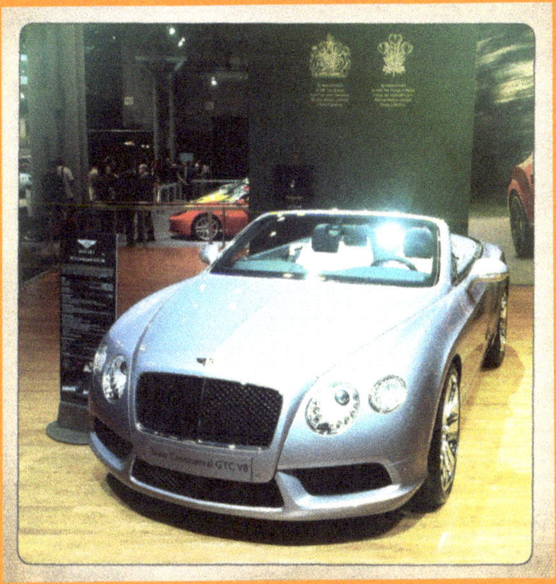

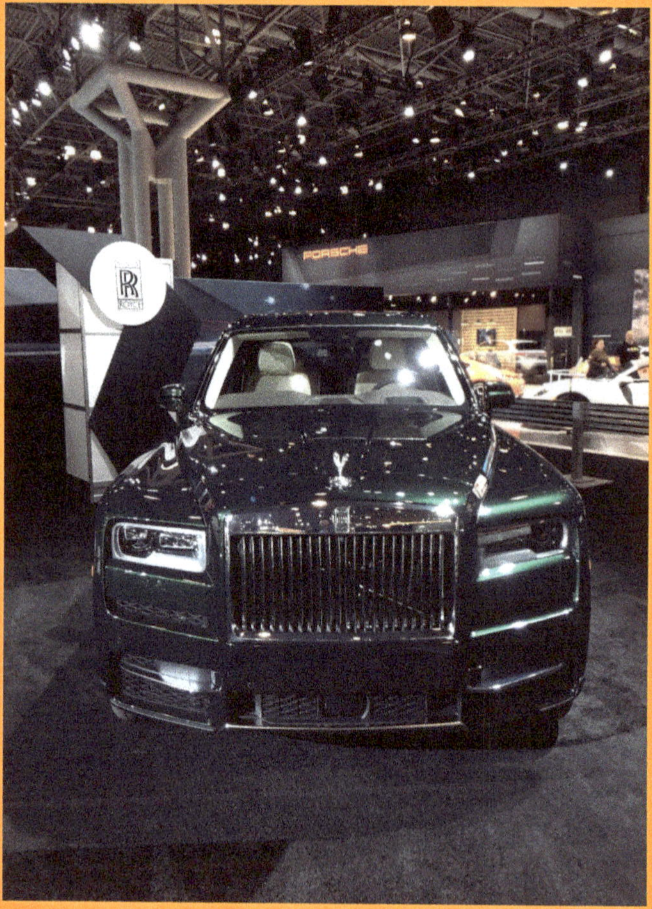
PORSCHE

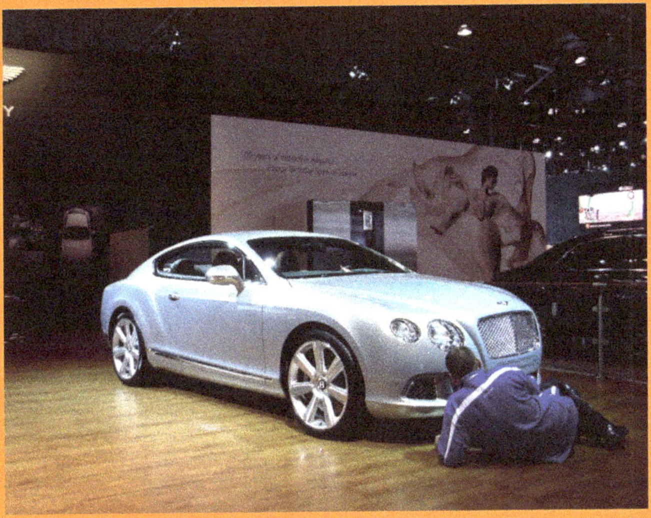

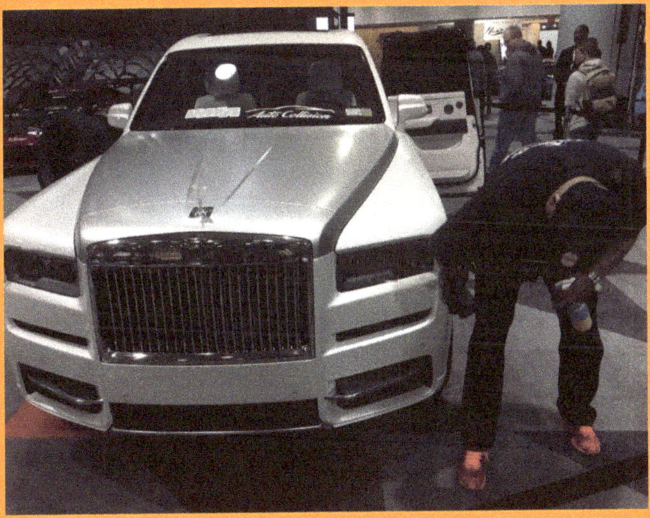
Auto Collision

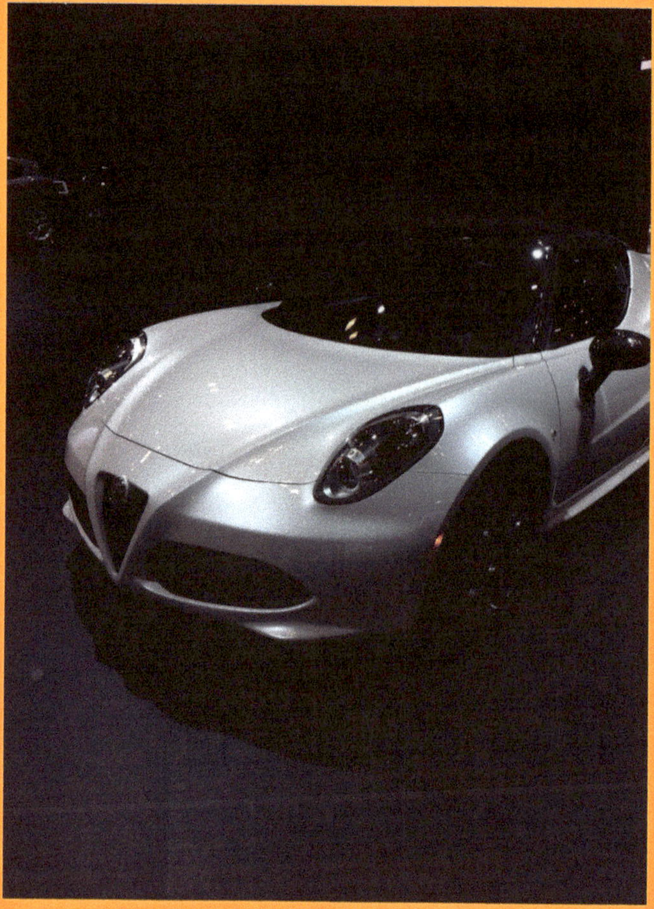

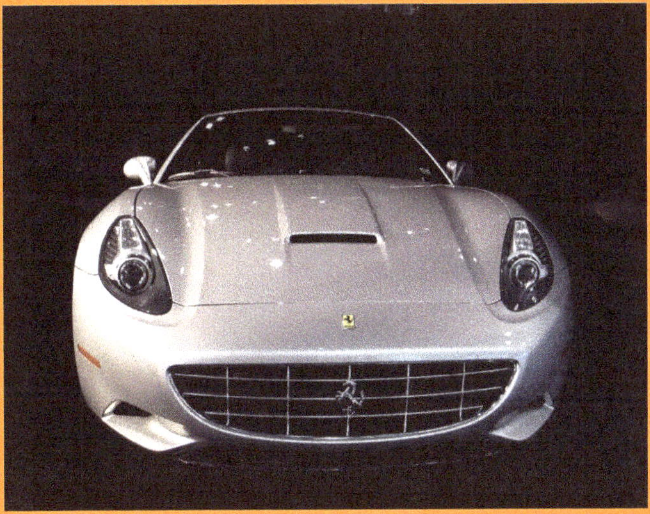

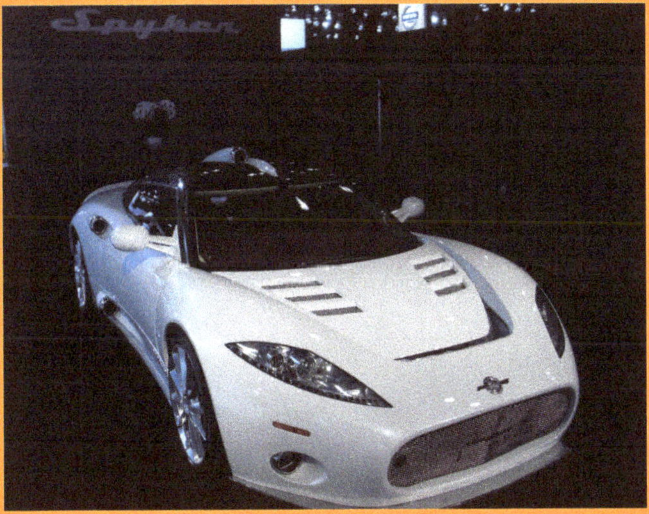

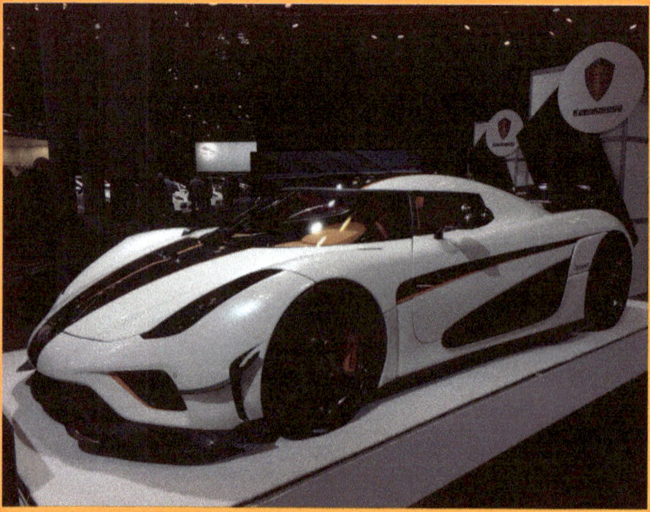

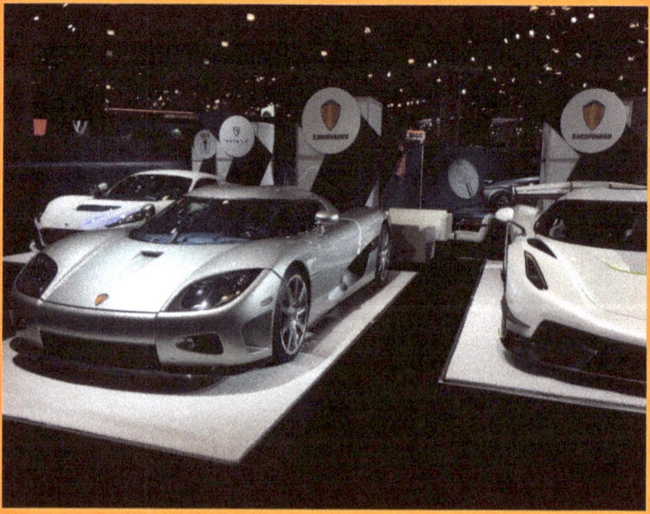

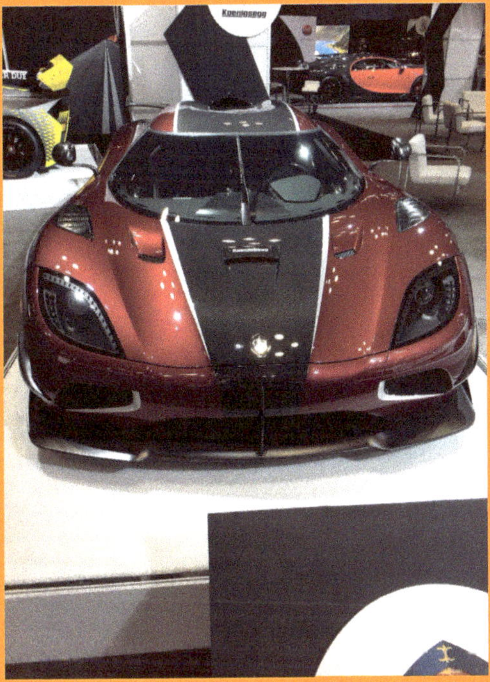

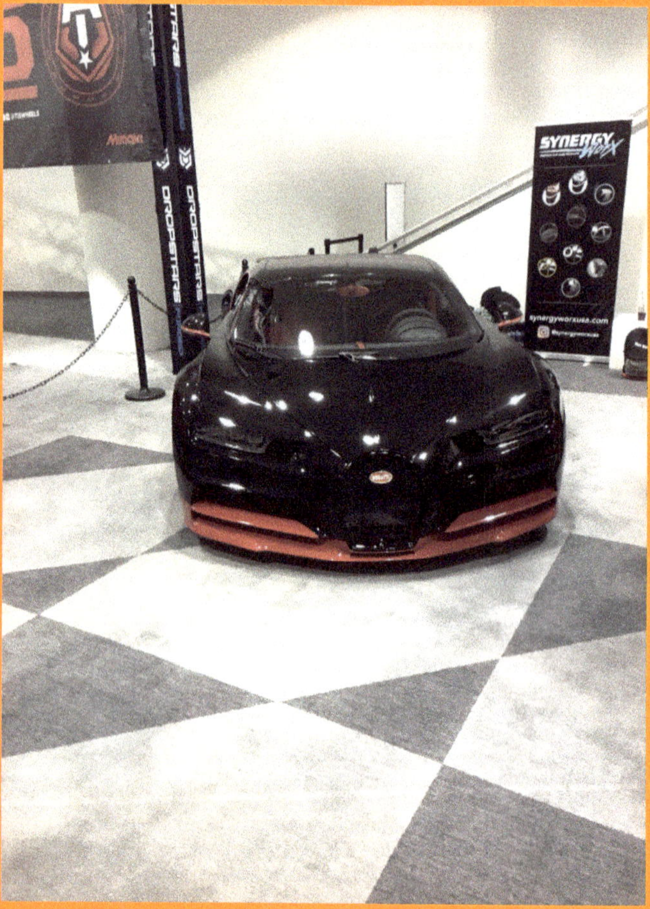
DROPSTARS
DROPSTARS
SYNERGY
synergyworxusa.com

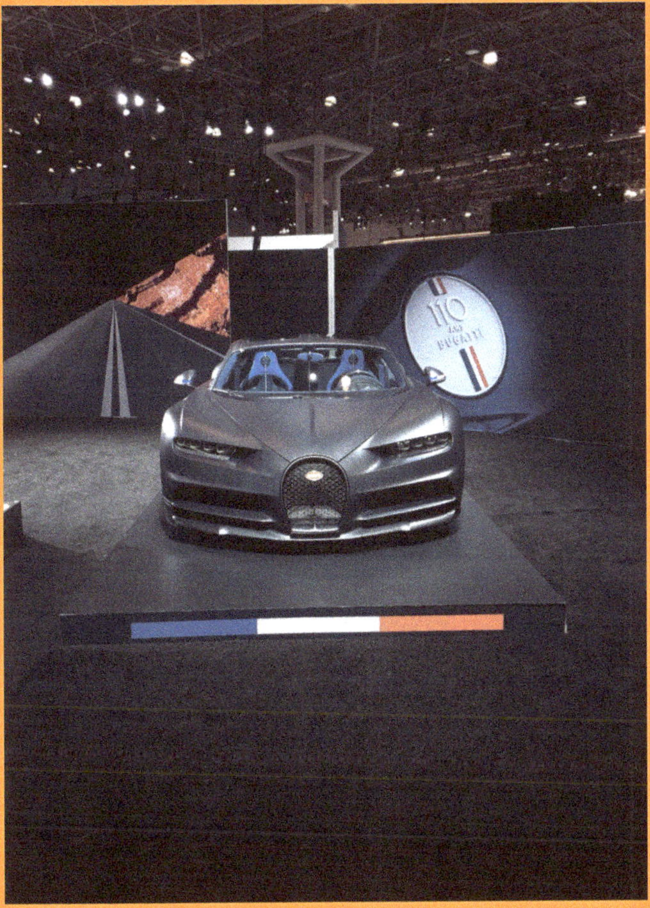
110

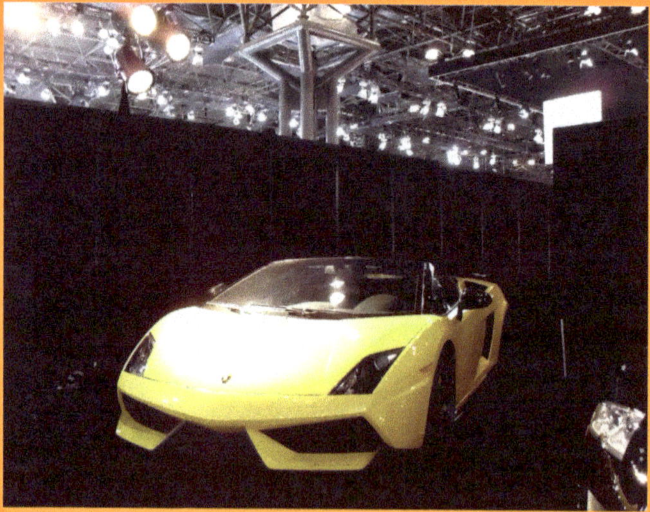

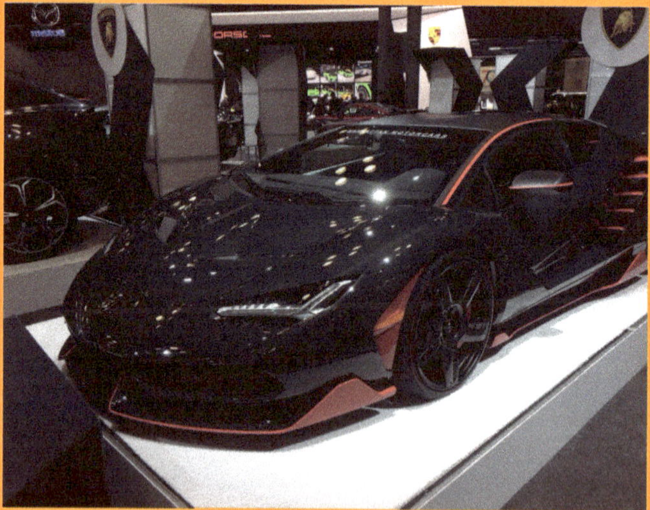

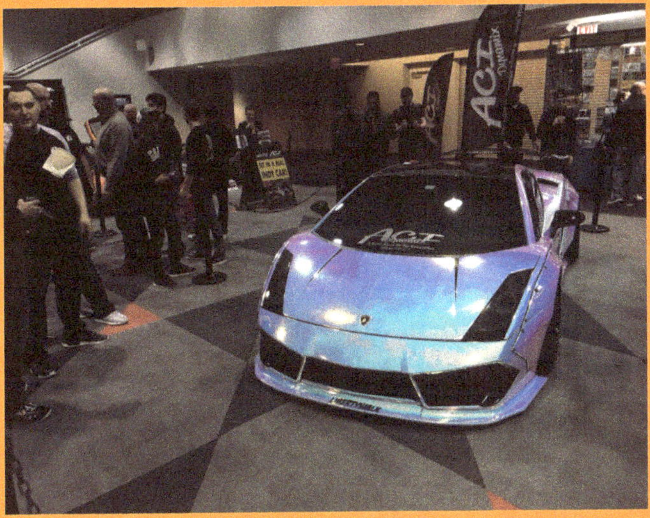

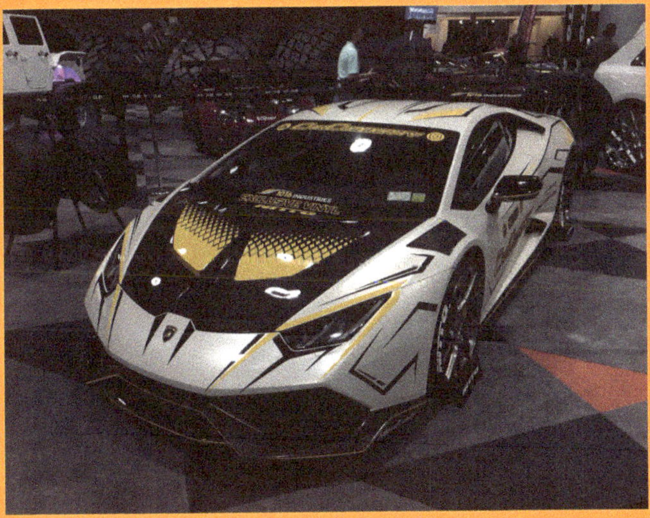

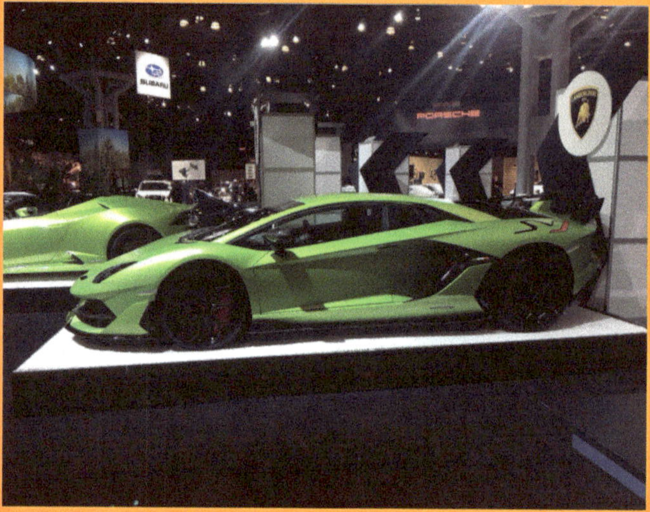
SUBARU
PORSCHE

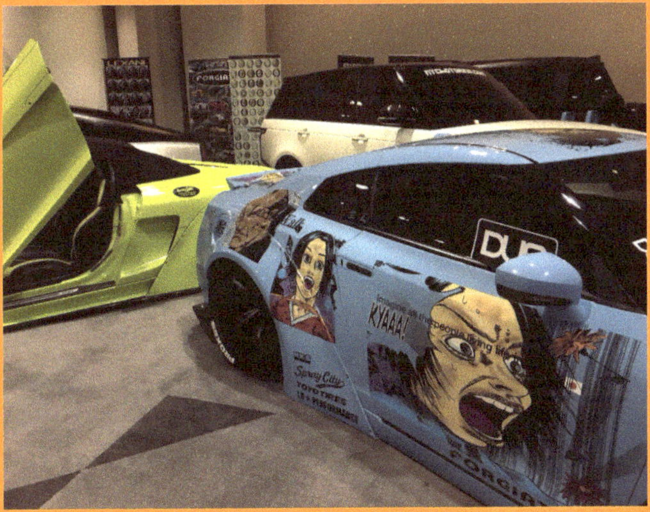
KYAAA!

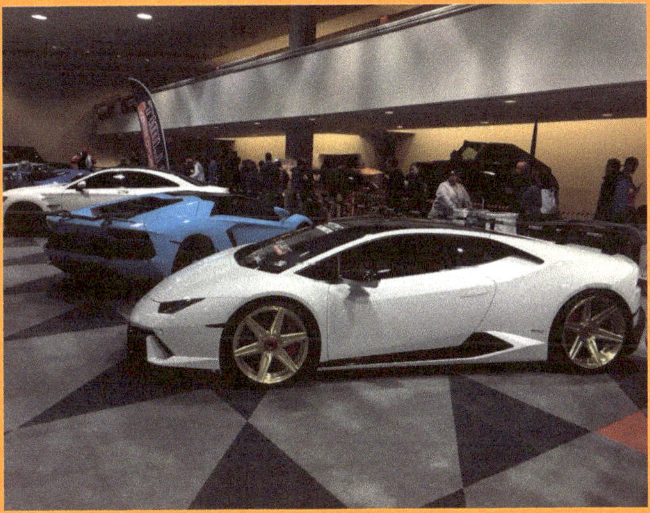

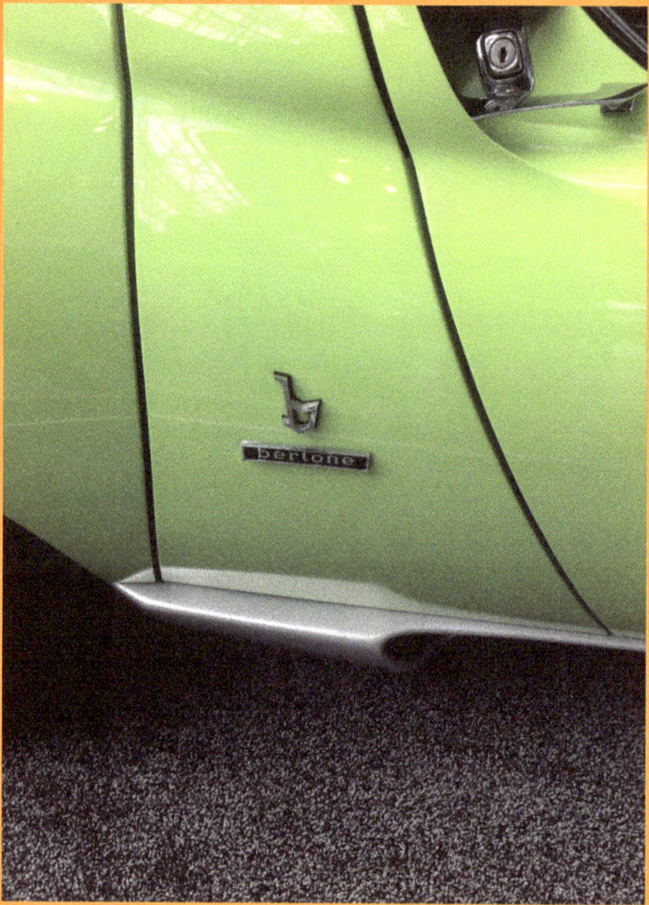
bertone

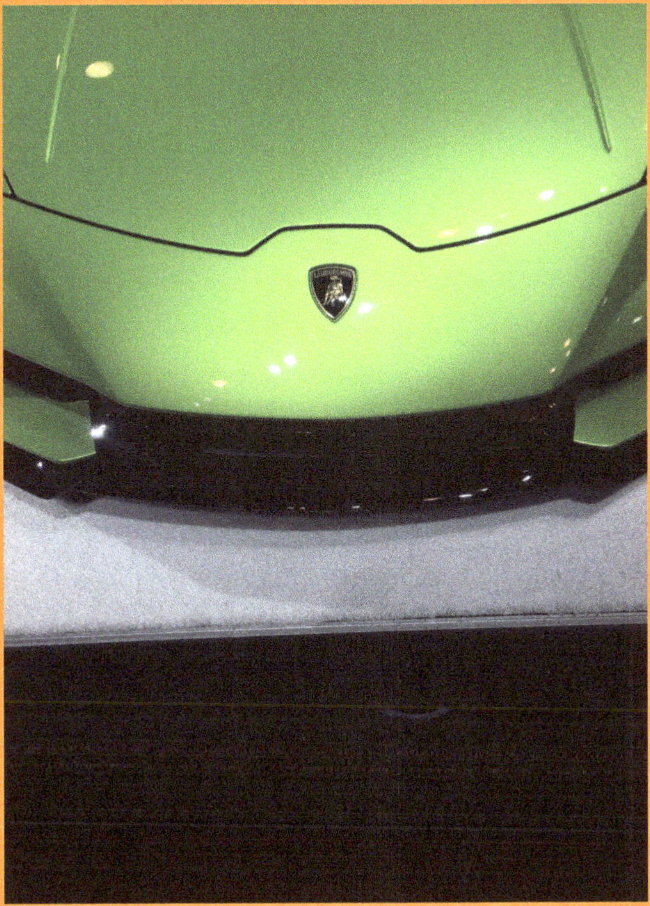

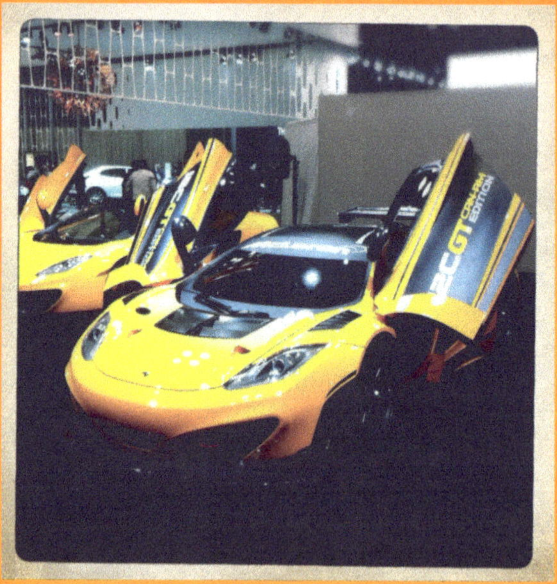
GT
EDITION

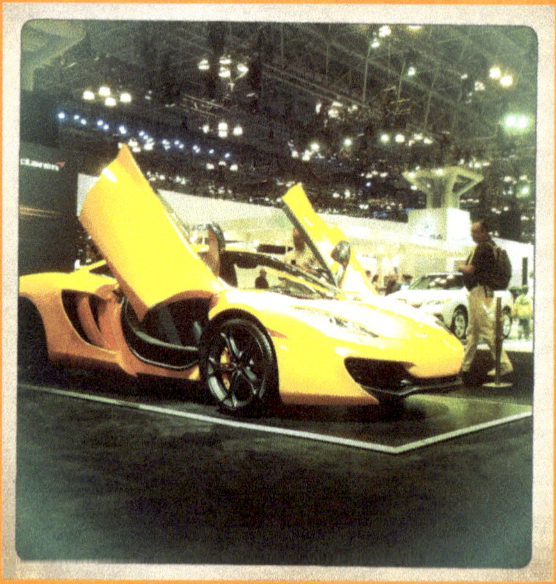

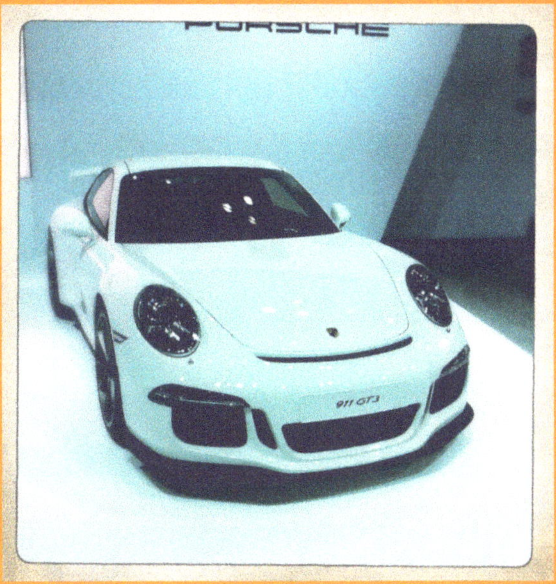
911 GT3

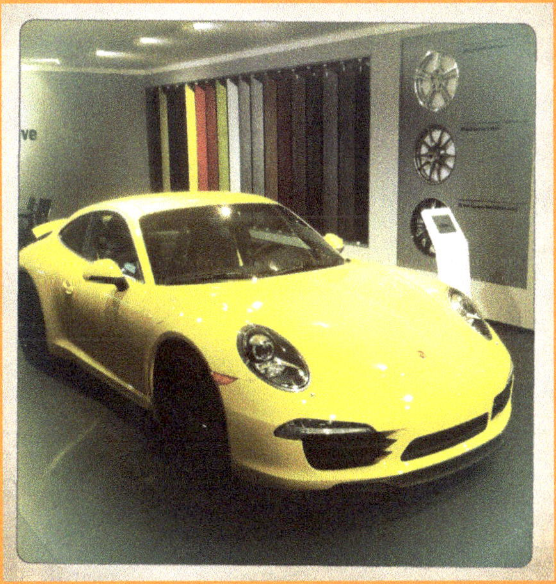

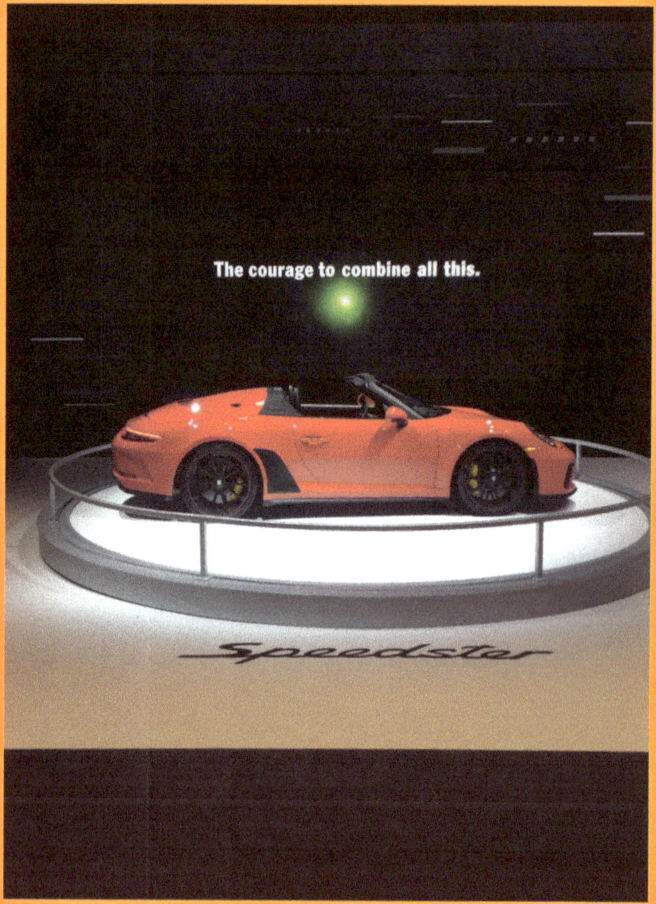
The courage to combine all this.
Speedster

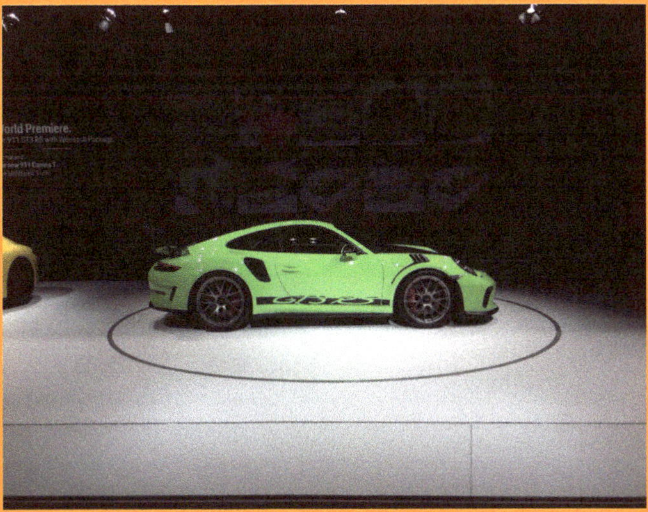
orld Premiere.

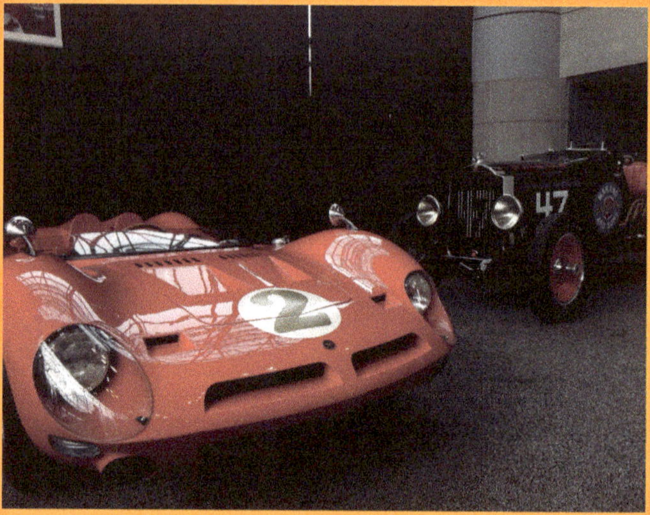
2
47

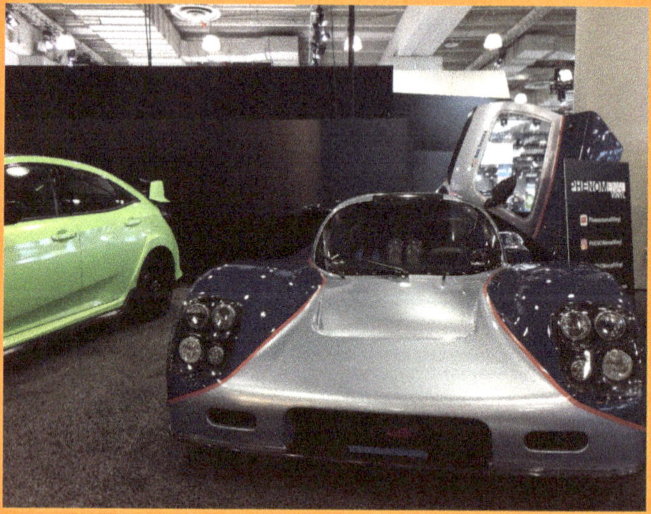

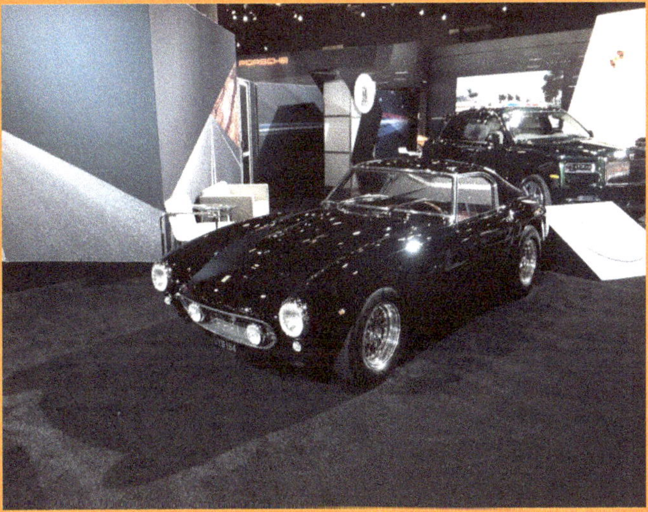

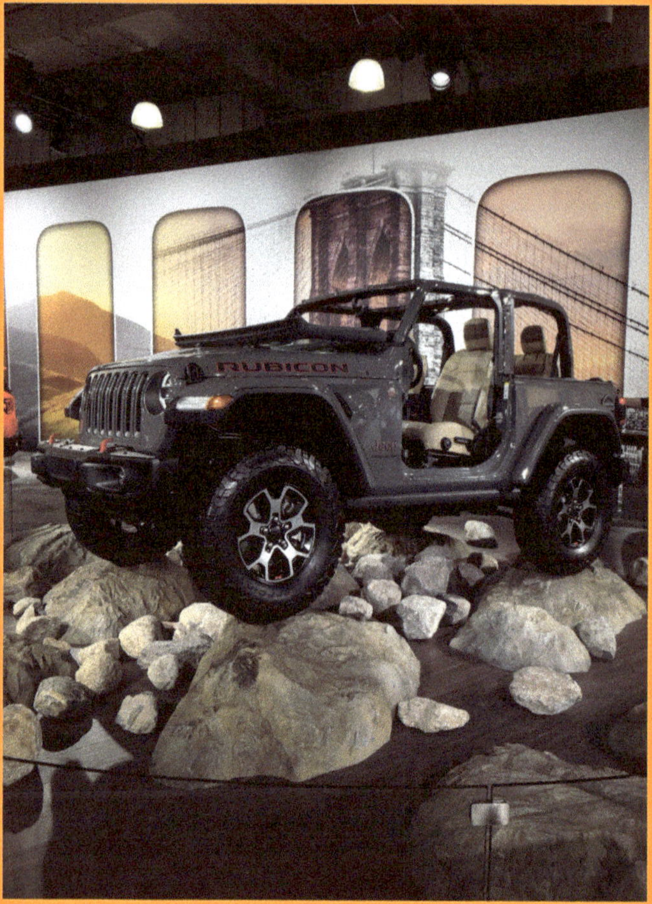
RUBICON

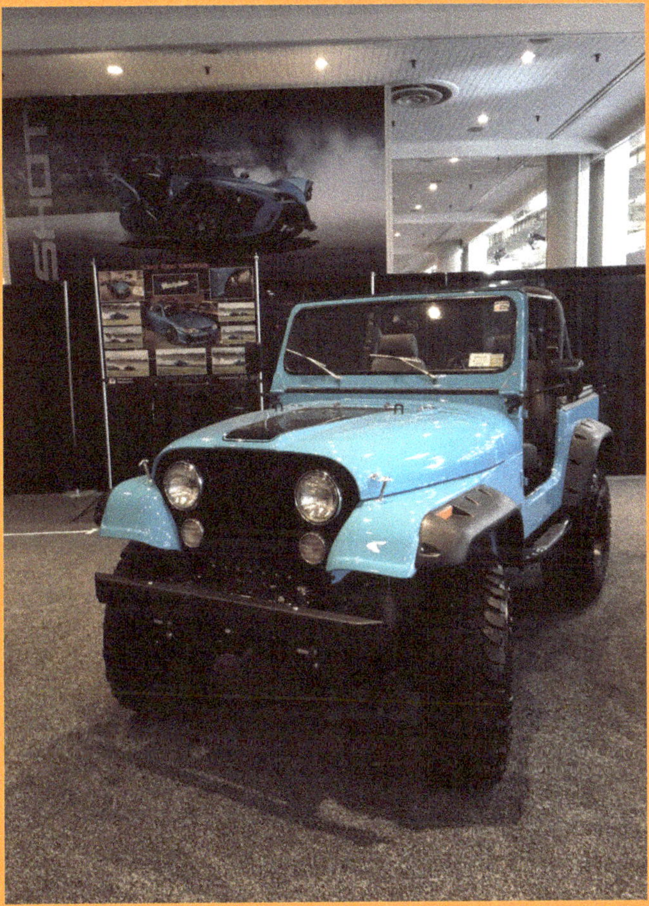

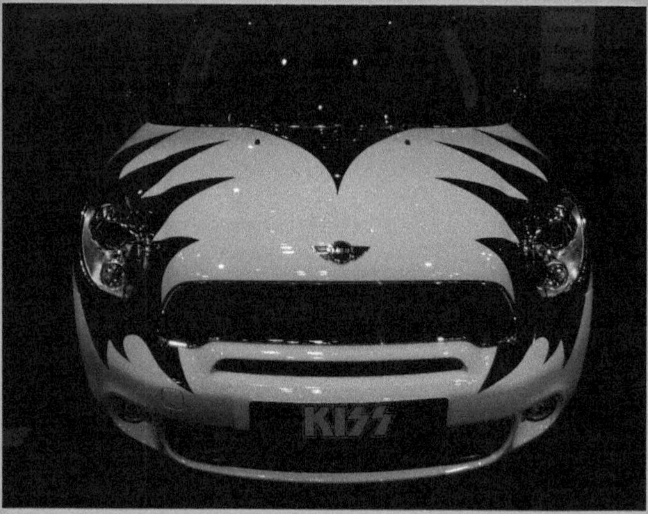
KISS

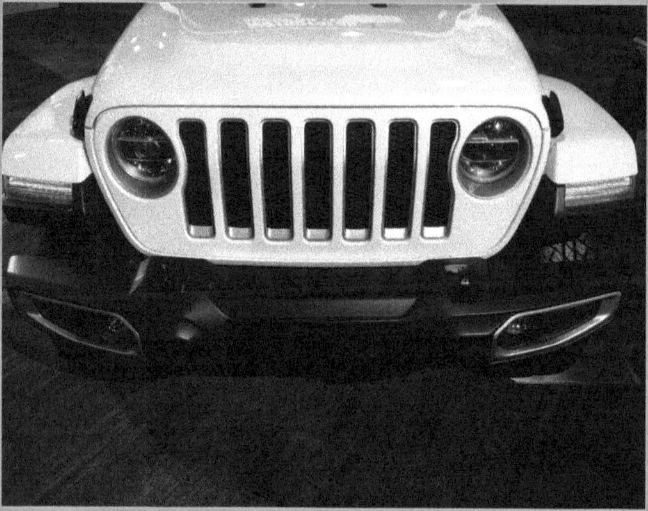

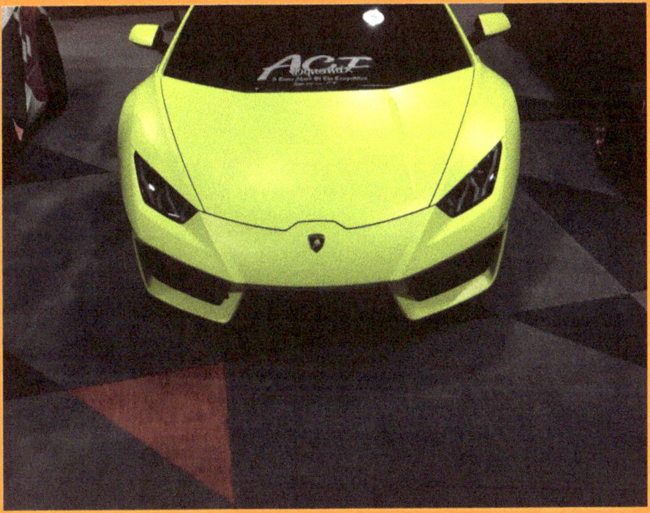
ACE

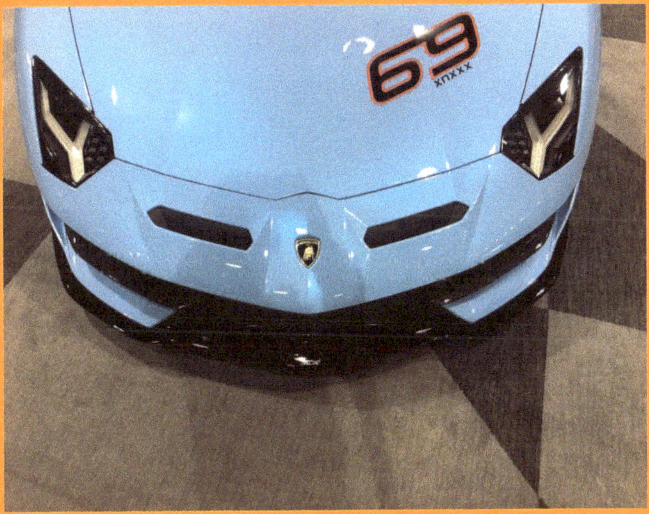
69

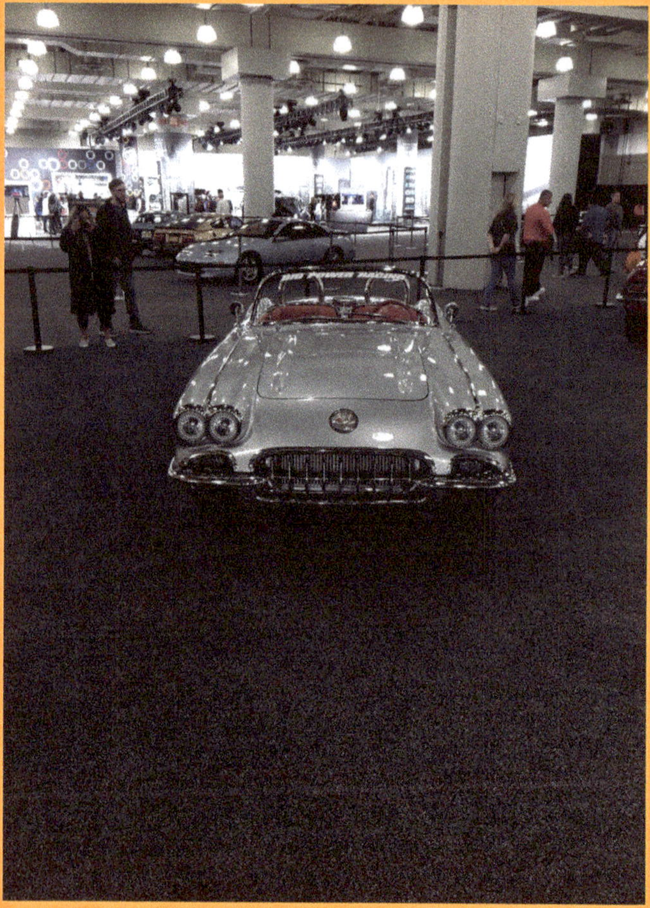

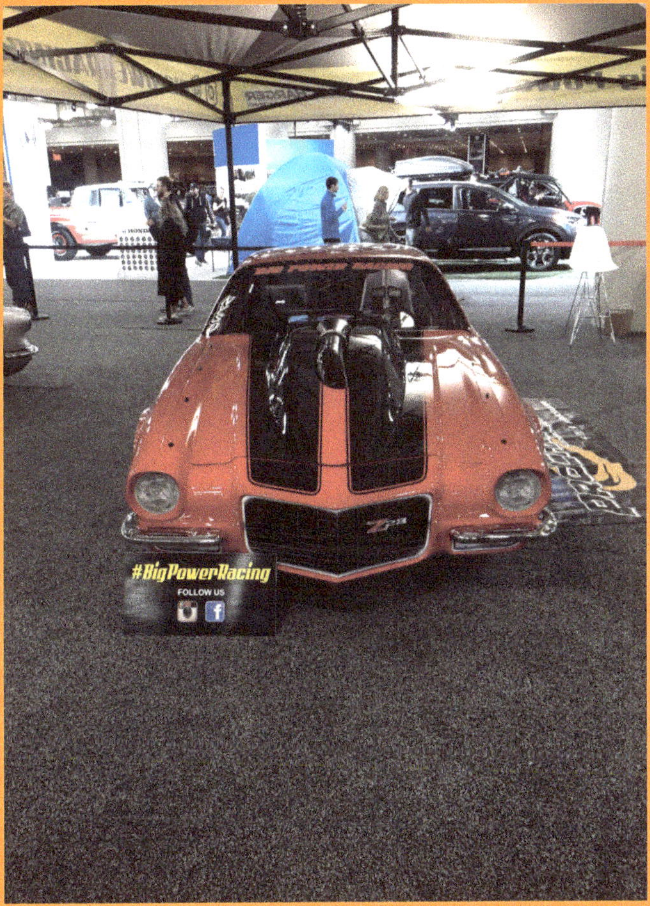
#BigPowerRacing
FOLLOW US

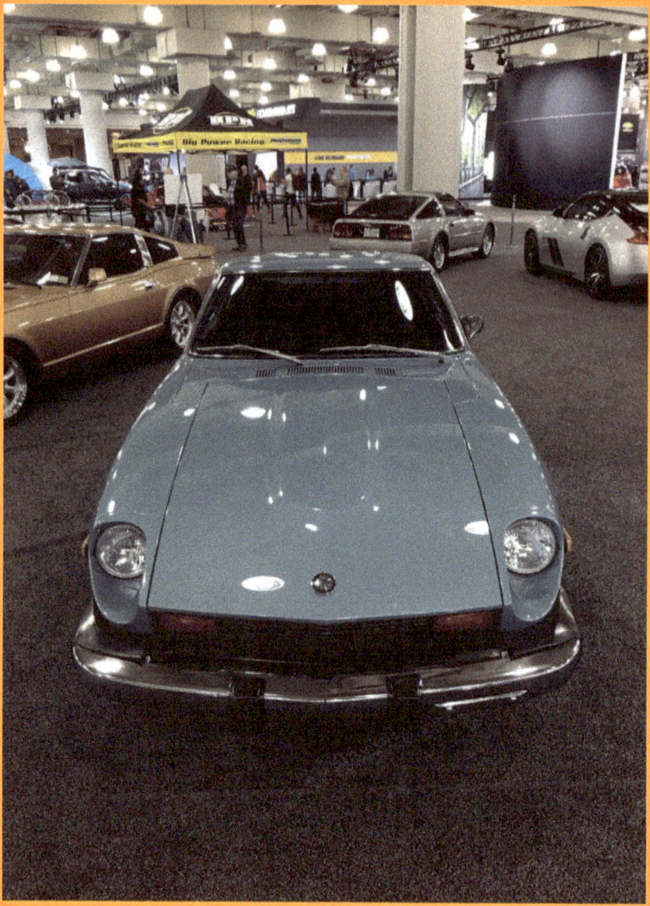
Big Power Racing

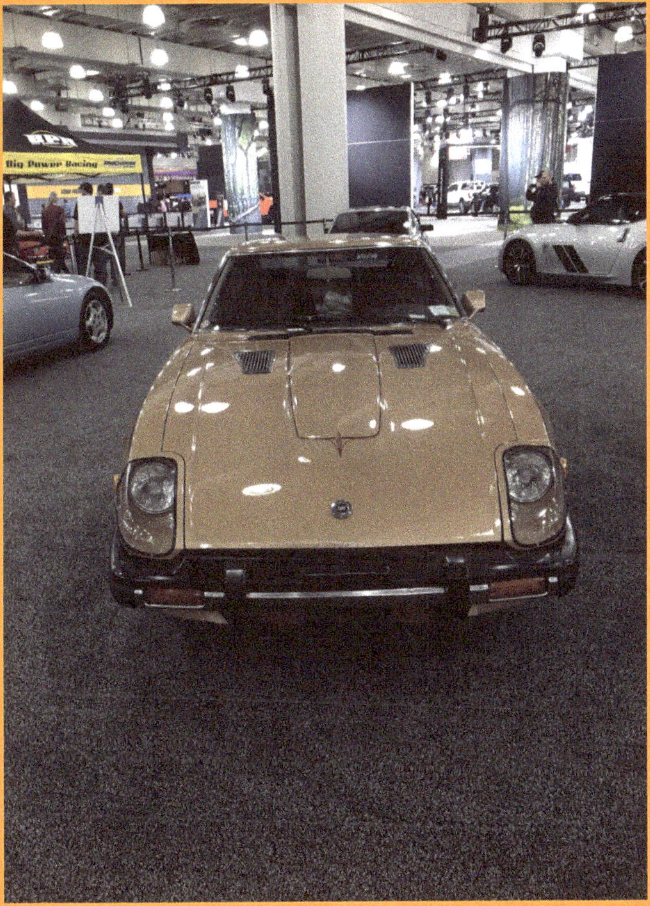
Big Power Racing

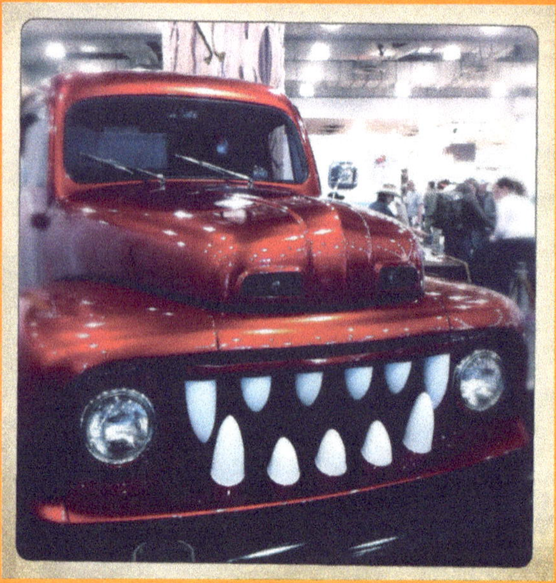

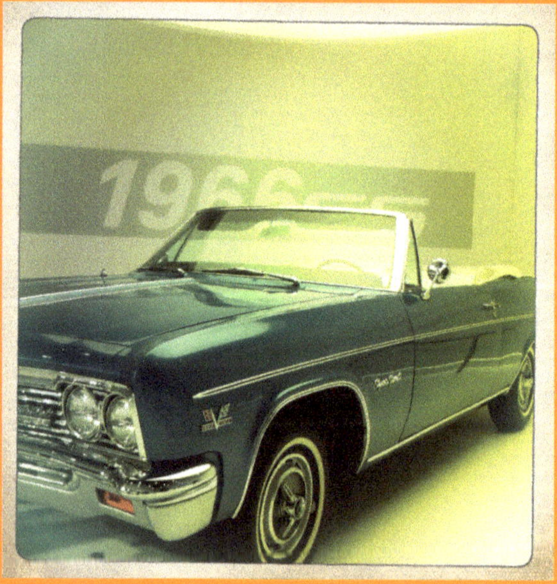

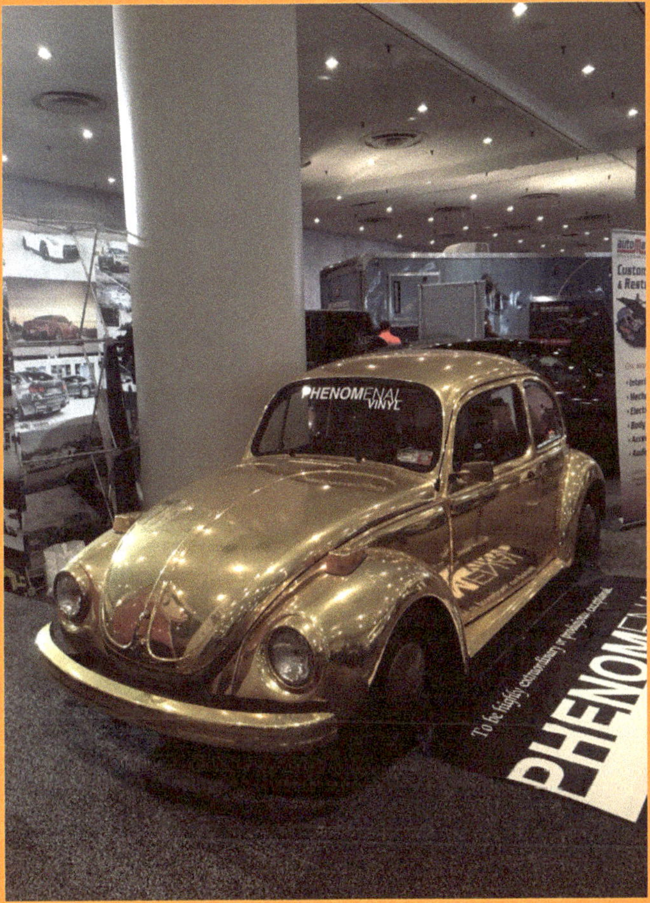
PHENOMENAL
VINYL

END

END

END

END

END

END

END

FAST DON'

FAST DON'T

E FAST DON'T

VE FAST DON'T ST

RIVE FAST DON'T STO

DRIVE FAST DON'T STOP

DRIVE FAST DON'T STOP

7

DRIVE FAST DON'T STOP

WWW.DRIVEFASTDONTSTOP.COM

AUTOMOTIVE PHOTO ARCHIVE
BY
MATTHEW JOCELYN

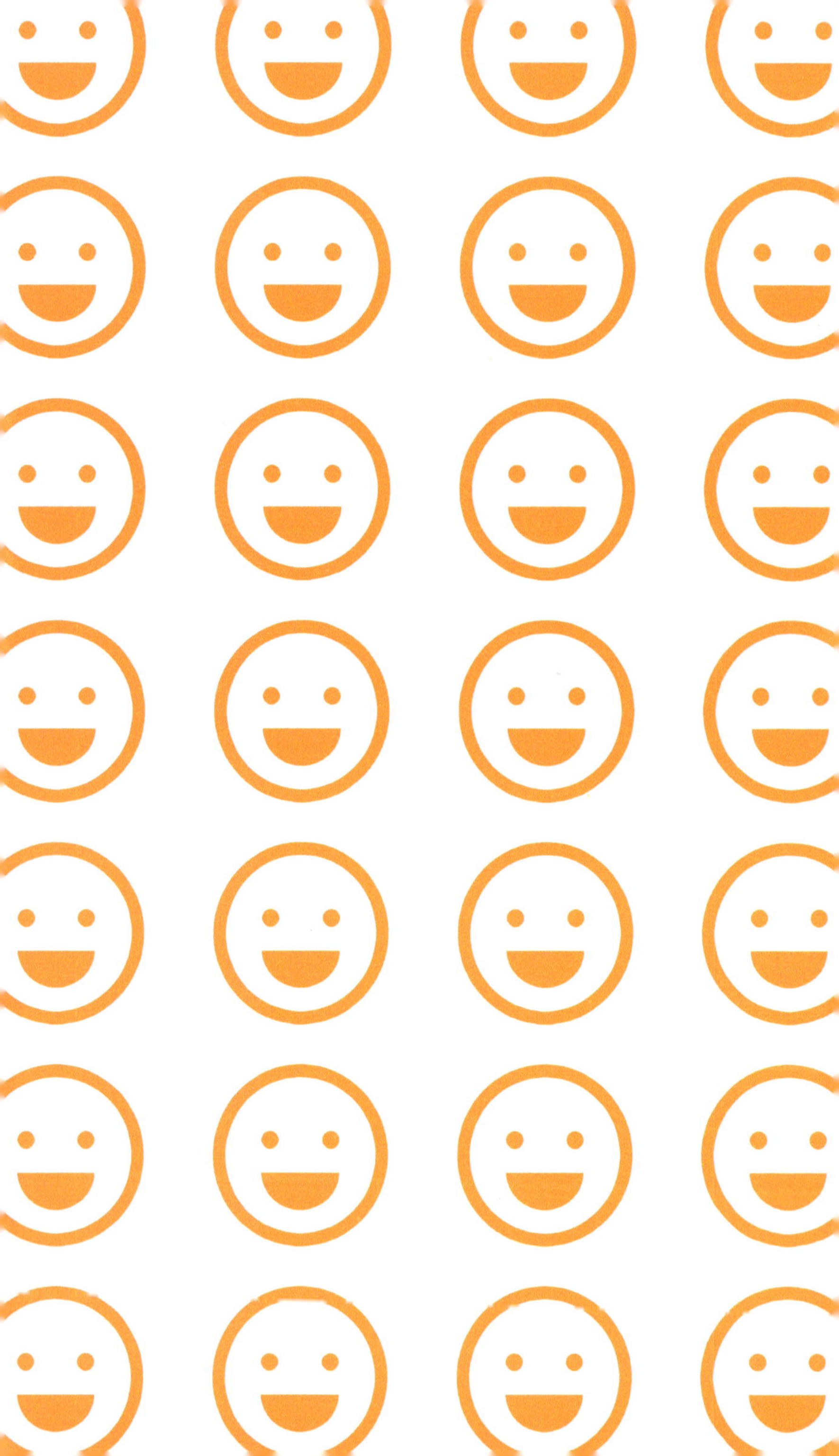

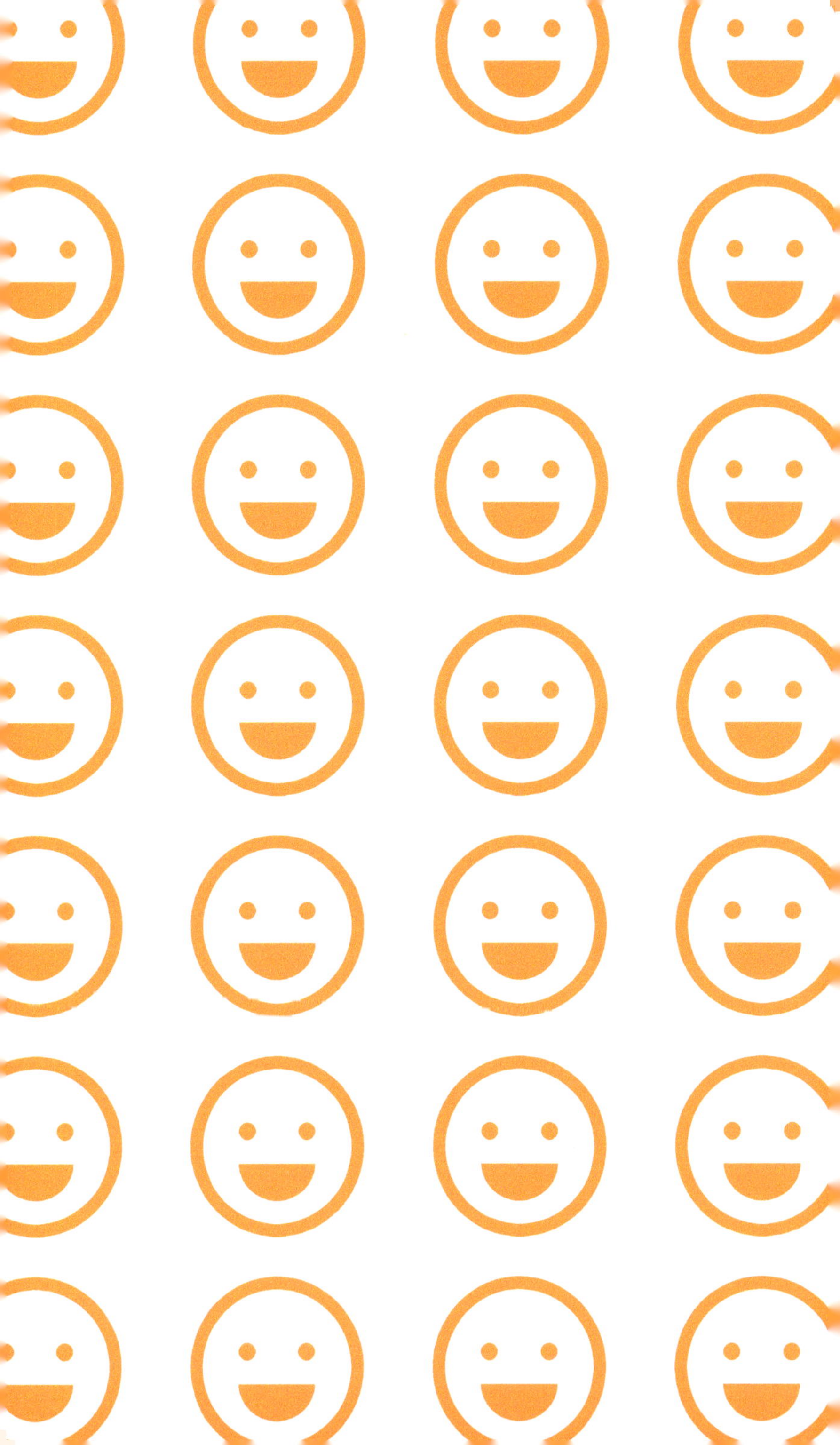

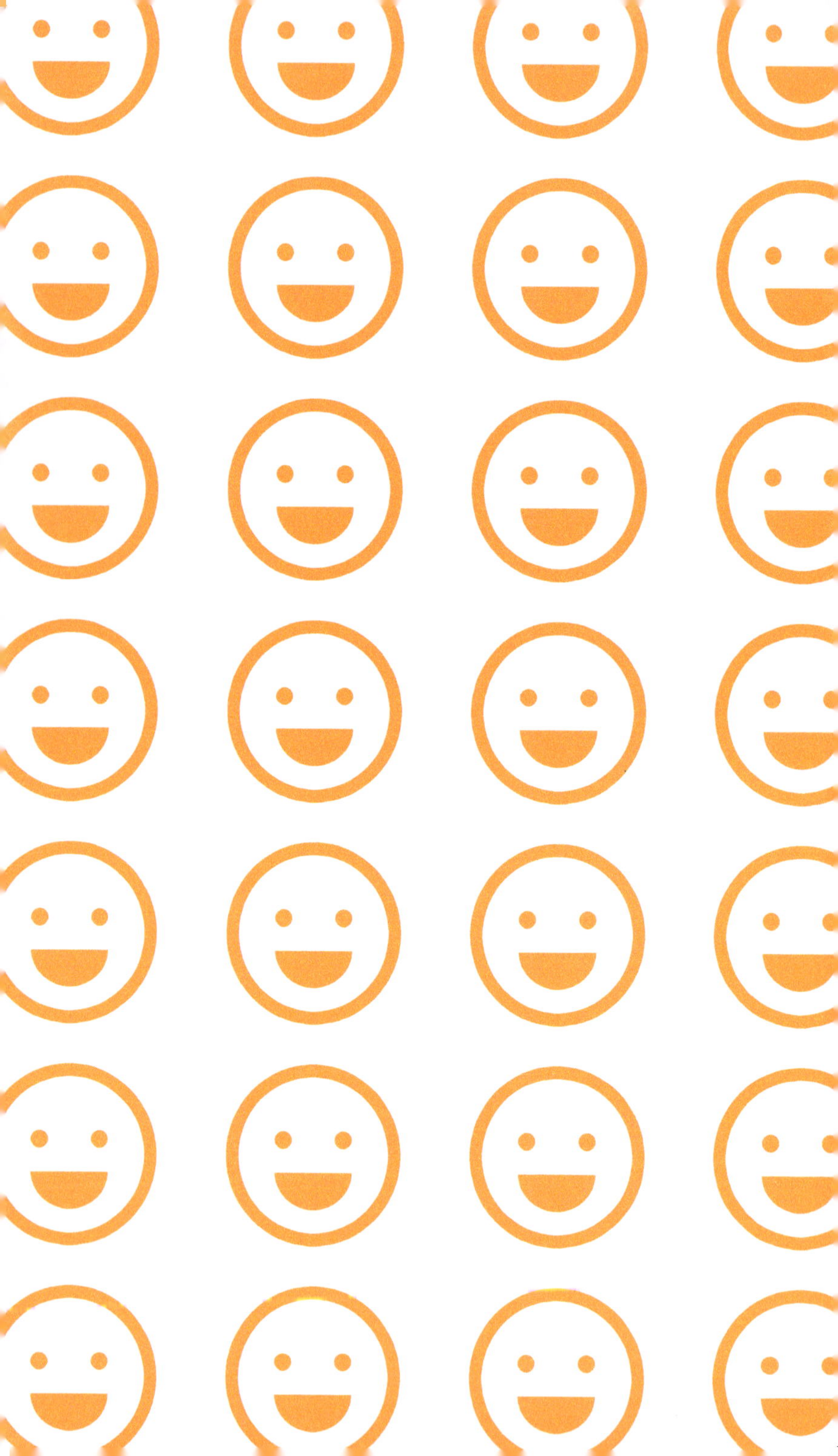

www.ingramcontent.com/pod-product-compliance
Lightning Source LLC
Chambersburg PA
CBHW041108280526
45792CB00010B/2341
* 9 7 9 8 8 8 1 4 4 5 4 6 1 *